MANAGING A NARCISSIST

"Navigating the Complex World of Narcissism: Strategies for Empowerment and Healing"

FRED K. FORTNER

TABLE OF CONTENT

<u>Preface</u>

<u>Introduction</u>

<u>Chapter 1: Understanding Narcissism</u>
1.1 Defining Narcissism
1.2 The Spectrum of Narcissistic Traits
1.3 Diagnosing Narcissistic Personality Disorder (NPD)
1.4 The Origins of Narcissism
1.5 Myths and Misconceptions About Narcissism

<u>Chapter 2: Recognizing Narcissistic Behavior</u>
2.1 Identifying Narcissistic Traits
2.2 Red Flags and Warning Signs
2.3 Covert vs. Overt Narcissism
2.4 Narcissistic Supply
2.5 Differentiating Between NPD and Other Personality Disorders

Chapter 3: The Impact of Narcissism

3.1 Narcissism in Relationships

3.2 Narcissism in the Workplace

3.3 The Toll on Family and Friends

3.4 Societal and Cultural Aspects

3.5 The Narcissistic Cycle of Abuse

Chapter 4: Coping and Self-Care

4.1 Self-Care Strategies for Dealing with a Narcissist

4.2 Setting Boundaries

4.3 Maintaining Emotional Health

4.4 Seeking Support

4.5 Practicing Patience and Empathy

Chapter 5: Strategies for Managing a Narcissist

5.1 Communication Techniques

5.2 Dealing with Manipulation

5.3 Conflict Resolution

5.4 Grey Rock Method

5.5 Using the "Broken Record" Approach

Chapter 6: Navigating Relationships

6.1 Romantic Partners

6.2 Family Members

6.3 Friends and Acquaintances

6.4 Co-Parenting with a Narcissist

Chapter 7: In the Workplace

7.1 Recognizing Narcissism in the Office

7.2 Dealing with a Narcissistic Boss

7.3 Managing Narcissistic Colleagues

7.4 Narcissism and Leadership

Chapter 8: The Recovery Journey

8.1 Leaving or Detaching from a Narcissist

8.2 Healing and Self-Discovery

8.3 Post-Narcissistic Stress Disorder (PNSD)

8.4 Rebuilding Relationships and Trust

Chapter 9: Professional Help and Interventions

9.1 Therapy and Counseling Options

9.2 Family Interventions

9.3 Legal Considerations

9.4 Support Groups and Resources

Chapter 10: Coping with Co-Parenting
10.1 Parenting Strategies with a Narcissistic Ex
10.2 The Impact on Children
10.3 Legal Custody and Co-Parenting Agreements
10.4 Emotional Support for Children

Chapter 11: The Journey to Empowerment
11.1 Self-Empowerment and Growth
11.2 Thriving Beyond Narcissism
11.3 Reclaiming Your Life

Chapter 12: Looking Ahead
12.1 The Future of Narcissism
12.2 Breaking the Cycle
12.3 Promoting Empathy and Mental Health

Conclusion

Preface

Dealing with a narcissist can be a formidable challenge, an intricate dance through a world where egos loom large, and empathy is in short supply. Narcissistic traits and behaviors can manifest in a variety of relationships, from personal to professional, and they often leave us grappling with confusion, emotional turmoil, and a profound sense of powerlessness.

As you hold this book in your hands, you're embarking on a journey—a journey that will take you deep into the heart of narcissism and equip you with essential tools for managing and coping with these complex individuals. "Managing a Narcissist" is more than a guide; it's your resource for understanding, surviving, and, in some cases, even thriving amidst narcissistic relationships.

This book is structured to provide you with a comprehensive understanding of narcissism and its various forms, offer practical strategies for navigating the narcissist's world, and empower you to reclaim your emotional well-being. The insights within these pages have been carefully crafted to help you regain control, foster healthy boundaries, and find your path to healing.

In the following chapters, you'll find a road map for dealing with narcissistic individuals, whether they're a family member, a partner, a coworker, or even yourself. We'll delve into the intricacies of narcissistic behavior and explore the most effective techniques for managing and mitigating its impact on your life. Throughout your journey, remember that understanding is your first step to empowerment, and knowledge is your greatest ally.

This book is for anyone who has ever grappled with the complexities of narcissism—those who have been affected by narcissists' behavior and those who may be seeking to transform themselves. It's an exploration of the human psyche, a guide to personal growth, and a source of healing. Most importantly, it's a testament to the strength of the human spirit.

As you read through the chapters ahead, I encourage you to reflect on your experiences and apply the strategies and insights to your unique circumstances. Together, we will navigate the challenging terrain of narcissism, illuminating a path toward self-discovery, resilience, and transformation.

So, with an open heart and a thirst for knowledge, let's embark on this journey of "Managing a Narcissist."

Introduction

In our intricate dance through the vast mosaic of human relationships, there exists a personality type that shines with a dazzling but often overpowering brilliance—the narcissist. These individuals have an extraordinary ability to dominate the emotional space, leaving others spellbound by their charm, charisma, and allure. However, beneath the surface of this captivating facade lies a complex and challenging world.

"Managing a Narcissist" is a guide through the labyrinthine landscapes of narcissism. It is a journey into the heart of darkness and light, exploring the enigmatic and compelling realm of narcissistic individuals—those whose narcissistic traits, behaviors, and personalities present unique challenges to those around them.

This book is not an exploration of psychology for psychologists, nor is it a critique of narcissistic traits. Instead, it is a guide for everyday people—partners, family members, friends, colleagues, and even those who recognize narcissistic traits within themselves. It is an illumination of the patterns, dynamics, and coping mechanisms that can enable you to navigate the labyrinth of narcissistic relationships.

In the chapters that follow, we will unravel the complexities of narcissism, seeking to understand what drives these individuals and why they often seem impervious to the emotions of those who revolve around them. We will delve into the intricacies of managing relationships with narcissists, offering strategies for emotional self-preservation, setting boundaries, and even fostering personal growth. Our journey is not only a tour through the territory of narcissism but a path toward self-discovery and empowerment.

The roadmap ahead guides us through the various facets of narcissism, starting with a foundational understanding of what narcissism is and the diverse forms it takes. We'll then explore the telltale signs and red flags of narcissistic behavior, equipping you with the insight to recognize it when you encounter it.

We'll venture into the depths of your emotions as we examine the profound impact narcissistic relationships can have on your mental health and well-being. You'll discover coping strategies to manage the emotional turmoil and emerge stronger and more resilient.

Setting boundaries is a central theme in our journey, and we'll provide you with practical guidance on how to establish, maintain, and enforce these vital barriers. This is a journey towards balance, enabling you to find your footing in the narcissist's world without losing your own identity.

The chapters that follow offer insights into dealing with specific types of narcissists you may encounter in your life—whether they be partners, family members, or coworkers. You'll learn about managing conflicts, building support networks, and even employing strategies for personal growth.

This book is not just about managing narcissists in your life; it's about managing your life when faced with narcissists. It's a beacon to guide you out of the storm, through treacherous waters, and into the calm harbor of self-awareness and empowerment. Each chapter presents an opportunity for understanding, reflection, and transformation.

As you embark on this journey through "Managing a Narcissist," remember that knowledge is your greatest ally. It's the lantern that illuminates the path ahead. In your hands, you hold the key to unraveling the mysteries of narcissism, rediscovering your inner strength, and forging your own path to healthier and more fulfilling relationships.

So, with an open heart and a quest for understanding, let us begin this expedition into the depths of narcissism and the heights of resilience, with the goal of emerging as a more empowered, balanced, and self-assured individual.

Chapter 1: Understanding Narcissism

1.1 Defining Narcissism

Narcissism, a term derived from Greek mythology, is a multifaceted personality trait or psychological construct that has intrigued scholars, psychologists, and the public for decades. To effectively manage and navigate relationships with narcissistic individuals, we must begin with a clear definition of narcissism.

Narcissism is, at its core, characterized by an excessive focus on oneself and a grandiose sense of self-importance. Individuals with narcissistic tendencies display a pervasive pattern of behavior marked by a strong desire for admiration and a lack of empathy for others. In essence, narcissism represents an unbalanced preoccupation with one's own needs, desires, and self-image.

While narcissism exists along a spectrum, with healthy self-esteem at one end and Narcissistic Personality Disorder (NPD) at the extreme other, there are several common traits and behaviors that are indicative of narcissism:

Grandiosity: Narcissistic individuals often harbor an exaggerated sense of their own abilities, achievements, and importance. They may fantasize about their limitless success and power, even when their actual accomplishments do not align with these fantasies.

Need for Admiration: Seeking constant praise, admiration, and validation from others is a hallmark of narcissism. They require this external affirmation to maintain their inflated self-image.

Lack of Empathy: Empathy, or the ability to understand and share the feelings of others, is frequently lacking in narcissistic individuals. They are more likely to exploit others for their own gain rather than express genuine compassion.

Manipulative Behavior: Narcissists are skilled manipulators. They use charm and charisma to influence those around them, often for personal advantage.

Fragile Self-Esteem: Despite their grandiose façade, narcissists often have fragile self-esteem that is easily wounded. They react strongly to criticism and may become defensive or aggressive in response.

The Narcissistic Continuum

It's essential to note that narcissism exists on a continuum. Not everyone who exhibits narcissistic traits or behaviors necessarily has Narcissistic Personality Disorder (NPD). Understanding the spectrum of narcissism helps us differentiate between individuals with healthy self-esteem and those with more pathological narcissistic tendencies.

By defining narcissism as a preoccupation with the self, a need for admiration, and a lack of empathy, we can begin to grasp the core characteristics that underpin narcissistic behavior. In the sections that follow, we will explore this spectrum more thoroughly, diagnose NPD, delve into the origins of narcissism, dispel myths and misconceptions, and, ultimately, provide practical guidance on managing relationships with narcissistic individuals.

1.2 *The Spectrum of Narcissistic Traits*

Narcissism, as a psychological construct, is not a one-size-fits-all phenomenon. It exists along a spectrum, ranging from individuals with healthy self-esteem to those with

Narcissistic Personality Disorder (NPD). This spectrum reflects the degree and intensity of narcissistic traits an individual may possess.

Understanding this spectrum is crucial in identifying and managing narcissistic traits in yourself and others. Let's explore the various levels of narcissistic traits:

1. Healthy Narcissism:

At the lower end of the spectrum, we find what is often referred to as "healthy narcissism." This term may sound paradoxical, but it reflects the essential components of a positive self-esteem and self-worth. Healthy narcissism includes elements such as self-confidence, self-respect, and a healthy sense of self-importance. People with these traits have a balanced perspective of their abilities, achievements, and the world around them. They can accept criticism, empathize with others, and maintain fulfilling relationships.

2. Normal Narcissism:

Moving slightly up the spectrum, we encounter "normal narcissism." This level includes individuals who possess some narcissistic traits but can manage them effectively in various life situations. These traits may occasionally surface, such as seeking admiration or being sensitive to criticism, but they don't dominate the individual's personality. It's normal for people to have moments of self-focus or desire for praise, especially in competitive or achievement-oriented contexts.

3. Atypical Narcissism:

Further along the spectrum, we enter the realm of "atypical narcissism." This category includes individuals who exhibit more noticeable narcissistic traits but may not meet the criteria for Narcissistic Personality Disorder. They often display heightened self-importance, grandiosity, and a constant need for admiration. While they can engage in social relationships and show empathy, these tendencies may disrupt their interactions with others.

4. <u>Pathological Narcissism:</u>
At the far end of the spectrum is "pathological narcissism." This is where we find individuals with Narcissistic Personality Disorder (NPD). People with NPD exhibit pervasive, inflexible narcissistic traits that significantly impair their functioning in various areas of life. Their sense of entitlement, lack of empathy, manipulative behavior, and constant need for admiration often lead to unstable relationships, work-related issues, and emotional distress.

Understanding the narcissistic spectrum is vital because it helps us distinguish between normal self-esteem and traits associated with narcissism that can cause interpersonal difficulties. It also assists in recognizing when narcissistic traits may escalate into a more severe disorder like NPD.

1.3 Diagnosing Narcissistic Personality Disorder (NPD)

Diagnosing a personality disorder is a complex process that requires careful evaluation by a mental health professional. Narcissistic Personality Disorder (NPD) is no exception. In this section, we will explore the criteria and procedures used to diagnose NPD.

1.3.1 Diagnostic Criteria for NPD:

The American Psychiatric Association's Diagnostic and Statistical Manual of Mental Disorders (DSM-5) provides specific criteria that must be met for a diagnosis of Narcissistic Personality Disorder. These criteria include:

Grandiosity: An exaggerated sense of self-importance and achievement, coupled with fantasies of unlimited success, power, brilliance, beauty, or ideal love.

Need for Admiration: A constant need for admiration and an expectation of special treatment.

Lack of Empathy: A significant lack of empathy, shown through an inability to recognize or identify with others' feelings and needs.

Interpersonal Exploitation: Exploitative behavior in relationships, taking advantage of others to achieve personal goals.

Envy and Belief Others are Envious: Persistent envy of others or the belief that others are envious of them.

Arrogance and Haughtiness: Display of arrogant, haughty behaviors or attitudes.

1.3.2 Clinical Evaluation:

Diagnosis of NPD is typically conducted by a licensed mental health professional, such as a psychiatrist, psychologist, or clinical social worker. The assessment process includes:

Clinical Interviews: The professional conducts in-depth interviews to understand the individual's thoughts, feelings, and behaviors, with a focus on narcissistic traits and their impact on daily life.

Psychological Testing: Standardized tests and self-report questionnaires may be administered to gather more information about the individual's personality and emotional state.

Gathering Information: Information is gathered from multiple sources, such as family members, friends, or partners, to gain a comprehensive view of the individual's behavior and its effects on relationships.

1.3.3 Differential Diagnosis:

NPD can sometimes be mistaken for other mental health conditions, particularly other personality disorders. Differential diagnosis aims to distinguish NPD from conditions like Borderline Personality Disorder, Antisocial Personality Disorder, or Histrionic Personality Disorder, as they may share some overlapping traits.

1.3.4 Challenges in Diagnosing NPD:

Diagnosing NPD can be challenging for several reasons:

Lack of Self-awareness: Individuals with NPD often lack self-awareness about their condition, making it difficult for them to seek help voluntarily.

Co-occurring Conditions: NPD frequently co-occurs with other mental health issues, such as depression or substance abuse, which can complicate the diagnosis.

Stigmatization and Denial: The stigma associated with personality disorders may lead to denial or resistance to diagnosis.

<u>1.3.5 *The Role of Diagnosis:*</u>

A formal diagnosis of NPD is essential for several reasons:

Treatment Planning: Diagnosis guides the development of an appropriate treatment plan tailored to the individual's needs.

Understanding and Compassion: A diagnosis fosters understanding and empathy in the family, friends, and partners of those with NPD.

Legal and Therapeutic Considerations: In some cases, a diagnosis may be relevant for legal or therapeutic reasons.

Recognizing and diagnosing Narcissistic Personality Disorder is a crucial step toward effective management and treatment. Later on, we will explore strategies for managing and interacting with individuals who exhibit narcissistic traits, whether or not they have received a formal diagnosis of NPD.

1.4 The Origins of Narcissism

Narcissism doesn't emerge in a vacuum but rather evolves through a complex interplay of genetic, environmental, and developmental factors. Understanding the origins of narcissism is crucial for gaining insight into why some individuals exhibit narcissistic traits and how these traits manifest. Here, we explore the various factors contributing to the development of narcissism.

1.4.1 Genetic Predisposition:

Research suggests that narcissism may have a genetic component. Certain genes may predispose individuals to exhibit narcissistic traits. Studies involving twins have shown that narcissism can be hereditary, with identical twins more likely to share narcissistic traits than fraternal twins.

1.4.2 Environmental Influences:

Environmental factors play a significant role in shaping narcissistic traits. Early childhood experiences, family dynamics, and parenting styles all contribute to the development of narcissism. Children raised in environments where they were excessively praised or, conversely, deprived of attention and affection, may be more prone to developing narcissistic traits as they seek external validation and approval.

1.4.3 Cultural and Societal Influences:

Cultural and societal factors also impact the prevalence of narcissism. In today's world, where self-promotion and individualism are highly encouraged, narcissistic traits may be more prevalent. The constant exposure to social media and celebrity culture can further nurture narcissistic tendencies.

1.4.4 Defense Mechanism:

For some individuals, narcissism can serve as a defense mechanism against underlying feelings of insecurity, inadequacy, or vulnerability. By overcompensating with grandiose self-perceptions and an attitude of superiority, they shield themselves from facing their deeper emotional issues.

Understanding these origins helps us to empathize with individuals demonstrating narcissistic traits and provides valuable insights for managing and interacting with them effectively. As we delve deeper into the topic of narcissism, we'll uncover how these origins influence the behavior of those with narcissistic traits.

1.5 Myths and Misconceptions About Narcissism

In our quest to comprehend narcissism and its multifaceted nature, it is equally important to dispel the myths and misconceptions that often cloud our understanding of this personality trait and disorder. This section addresses some of the prevalent misconceptions surrounding narcissism, allowing us to approach this subject with clarity and accuracy.

Myth 1: Narcissism is Just About Vanity:
One of the most common misconceptions is that narcissism solely revolves around vanity and excessive self-love. While self-admiration is an aspect of narcissism, it barely scratches the surface of this complex personality trait. Narcissism encompasses a spectrum of behaviors that go far beyond mere self-centeredness.

Myth 2: Narcissists Are Inherently Confident:
Many believe that narcissists are brimming with unwavering self-confidence. In truth, narcissism often masks profound insecurities and a fragile sense of self. Their arrogance and grandiosity serve as a defense mechanism against underlying feelings of inadequacy.

Myth 3: Narcissists Cannot Feel Empathy:
While narcissists may struggle with empathy and often display a lack of it, it is not accurate to say they are entirely devoid of this human capacity. The degree of empathy varies among narcissists, with some displaying occasional empathy and others demonstrating a chronic lack thereof.

Myth 4: Narcissism is Incurable:
Narcissism is a personality trait that exists on a spectrum, and not all narcissistic individuals meet the criteria for Narcissistic Personality Disorder (NPD). Moreover, with

the right therapeutic interventions and willingness on the part of the individual, change and personal growth are possible. However, it's essential to acknowledge that genuine change in those with NPD is often challenging.

Myth 5: Narcissists Are Easy to Spot:
In reality, identifying narcissistic individuals can be more complex than expected. While some display overt narcissistic behaviors, others are covert and mask their true nature effectively. Moreover, narcissistic traits can vary widely, making it challenging to pinpoint narcissism solely based on appearance or initial interactions.

Myth 6: Narcissism is Always Destructive:
Narcissism exists on a spectrum, and not all narcissistic traits are inherently destructive. In some situations, narcissistic characteristics can drive ambition and success. However, it is the extreme end of the narcissistic spectrum, particularly

Narcissistic Personality Disorder, that tends to result in harm to oneself and others.

By debunking these myths and misconceptions about narcissism, we create a more accurate foundation for understanding this complex personality trait and its associated disorders. With this clearer perspective, we can better navigate the nuanced landscape of narcissistic behavior and develop effective strategies for managing these relationships, which we will delve into in the following chapters.

Chapter 2: Recognizing Narcissistic Behavior

2.1 Identifying Narcissistic Traits

Recognizing narcissistic behavior is a crucial step in effectively managing relationships with individuals who exhibit narcissistic traits. By understanding the traits that are commonly associated with narcissism, you can better identify and respond to these behaviors. This section provides an in-depth exploration of key narcissistic traits:

2.1.1 Grandiosity and Exaggerated Self-Importance:

Narcissists often exhibit an inflated sense of self-importance. They may constantly exaggerate their achievements, talents, or importance. Identifying grandiose behavior can help you distinguish narcissistic individuals from others.

2.1.2 Lack of Empathy:

One hallmark of narcissism is a distinct lack of empathy. Narcissists may struggle to understand or care about the feelings and needs of others. They often prioritize their desires over the well-being of those around them.

2.1.3 Manipulative Behavior:

Narcissists may engage in manipulative tactics to maintain control or gain admiration. They can be skilled at emotional manipulation, guilt-tripping, or gaslighting, causing confusion and distress in their relationships.

2.1.4 Entitlement and Demandingness:

Narcissistic individuals often have a sense of entitlement, believing they deserve special treatment or privileges. They may make unreasonable demands and become agitated if these expectations are not met.

2.1.5 *Fragile Self-Esteem:*

Ironically, beneath the grandiose exterior, many narcissists harbor fragile self-esteem. Criticism or any perceived threat to their self-image can trigger extreme reactions, such as anger, defensiveness, or withdrawal.

2.1.6 *Need for Admiration:*

Narcissists crave constant admiration and validation from others. They seek attention and affirmation to boost their self-esteem, making them more prone to self-centered behavior.

2.1.7 *Competitive Nature:*

Narcissists often engage in intense competition, whether it's in professional or personal settings. They may strive to outperform others and be the center of attention.

2.1.8 Difficulty Accepting Criticism:

Constructive criticism is frequently met with resistance or hostility from narcissistic individuals. They struggle to accept feedback that challenges their self-perception.

By familiarizing yourself with these narcissistic traits, you'll be better equipped to recognize narcissistic behavior in your personal and professional relationships. This awareness is the first step toward effectively managing these interactions and maintaining your well-being. In the following sections, we will explore how to respond to narcissistic behavior and establish healthier boundaries.

2.2 Red Flags and Warning Signs

In this section, we will explore the specific red flags and warning signs that can help you identify narcissistic behavior in individuals. Recognizing these signs early is essential for effectively managing your interactions with narcissistic people and protecting your well-being.

2.2.1 *Charismatic at First Glance, Controlling Behind the Scenes:*

One common trait of narcissists is their initial charm and charisma. They can be exceptionally engaging and appealing when you first meet them. However, as you get to know them better, you may notice a controlling and manipulative side that becomes more evident.

2.2.2 *Love-Bombing and Idealization:*

Narcissists often engage in "love-bombing" during the early stages of a relationship. They shower you with affection, compliments, and gifts. While this may seem flattering, it's essential to recognize this behavior may not be genuine and can quickly turn into devaluation.

2.2.3 Frequent Displays of Arrogance:

Arrogance and condescension are typical narcissistic traits. Pay attention to individuals who frequently display these behaviors, especially if they belittle others or act as though they are above the rules.

2.2.4 Aversion to Criticism:

Narcissists have an extreme aversion to criticism and often react defensively or aggressively when confronted with their flaws or mistakes. They may deflect blame onto others or become highly reactive to even constructive feedback.

2.2.5 Emotional Manipulation and Gaslighting:

Narcissists are adept at emotional manipulation and gaslighting, which is a tactic used to make you doubt your own perceptions and memories. Be cautious if you find yourself consistently second-guessing your own feelings and experiences.

2.2.6 Inconsistent Behavior:

Narcissists may display highly inconsistent behavior. They can be warm and caring one moment and cold and dismissive the next. These mood swings can be disorienting for those around them.

2.2.7 Frequent Boundary Violations:

Narcissistic individuals often have a disregard for personal boundaries. They may intrude on your personal space, privacy, or emotional boundaries without regard for your comfort or consent.

2.2.8 Excessive Self-Centeredness:

Keep an eye out for excessive self-centeredness. Narcissists frequently monopolize conversations, making them primarily about themselves. They may show little genuine interest in your thoughts or feelings.

2.2.9 _Lack of Empathy and Emotional Support:_

If you notice a consistent lack of empathy and emotional support from someone in your life, it could be a sign of narcissistic behavior. They may struggle to understand or validate your emotions.

Understanding these red flags and warning signs is vital for safeguarding your emotional well-being when dealing with narcissistic individuals. By recognizing these early indicators, you can establish healthier boundaries and develop strategies for effectively managing such relationships.

2.3 Covert vs. Overt Narcissism

Understanding narcissistic behavior involves discerning between two primary presentations of narcissism: covert and overt narcissism. These distinctions are crucial in recognizing and comprehending the multifaceted nature of narcissistic traits and their impact on individuals and relationships.

Covert Narcissism: The Hidden Narcissist

Covert narcissism, often referred to as vulnerable narcissism, presents a different face of narcissistic behavior. Individuals with covert narcissism tend to be less conspicuous in their grandiosity and self-centeredness. Instead, they mask their narcissistic tendencies with a veneer of humility and even victimhood. Key characteristics of covert narcissism include:

Hypersensitivity: Covert narcissists are prone to feeling hurt or slighted by perceived criticisms or slights. They often respond to these perceived offenses with self-pity or passive-aggression.

Inferiority Complex: Unlike overt narcissists, who often project an air of superiority, covert narcissists frequently harbor deep-seated feelings of inferiority and self-doubt. Their narcissism serves as a defense mechanism against these inner insecurities.

External Validation: Covert narcissists seek external validation and reassurance, but they do so in subtler ways. They may fish for compliments, attention, or sympathy without appearing overtly self-absorbed.

Overt Narcissism: The Obvious Narcissist

Overt narcissism, sometimes referred to as grandiose narcissism, is the more recognizable face of narcissistic behavior. Individuals with overt narcissism tend to exhibit their self-centeredness prominently. Key characteristics of overt narcissism include:

Grandiosity: Overt narcissists often display an exaggerated sense of their own importance and may openly brag about their achievements and qualities.

Lack of Empathy: They frequently demonstrate a pronounced lack of empathy for the feelings and needs of others, using people as tools to serve their own ends.

Attention-Seeking: Overt narcissists are attention seekers. They aim to be the center of focus, and they may become frustrated or angry if they don't receive the admiration or attention they crave.

The Duality of Narcissism

It's important to note that narcissism isn't a one-size-fits-all personality trait. Many individuals exhibit a blend of covert and overt narcissistic tendencies, which can make recognition challenging. Moreover, the presentation of narcissism can change depending on the situation, which further complicates identification.

By understanding the differences between covert and overt narcissism, you'll be better equipped to recognize narcissistic traits in those around you. In the subsequent chapters, we'll explore strategies for dealing with both covert and overt narcissistic behaviors effectively, ensuring that you can navigate these challenging relationships with greater insight and success.

2.4 Narcissistic Supply

In the complex world of narcissistic behavior, the concept of "narcissistic supply" plays a pivotal role in understanding how narcissists feed their insatiable need for admiration, validation, and attention. Recognizing the dynamics of narcissistic supply is crucial for comprehending the behaviors of individuals with narcissistic traits and how they impact their relationships.

Narcissistic supply refers to the emotional sustenance and validation that narcissists constantly seek to maintain their fragile self-esteem and inflated self-image. It can manifest in various forms, including compliments, attention, admiration, and even fear or submission. Narcissistic individuals require a steady flow of this "supply" to uphold their grandiose self-concept.

Primary Sources of Narcissistic Supply

Admiration and Praise: Narcissists thrive on admiration and praise. They need to hear that they are exceptional, talented, or unique. This reinforces their belief in their own superiority.

Attention: Attention is a fundamental component of narcissistic supply. Narcissists often demand to be the center of attention in social situations and become irritated if the focus shifts away from them.

Validation: Narcissists seek validation for their opinions, ideas, and actions. They want others to confirm that they are always right and superior.

Control: Some narcissists derive supply from controlling and manipulating others. The feeling of dominance and power feeds their ego.

Submissiveness: In some cases, narcissists obtain supply from having others submit to their wishes. This can take the form of fear, compliance, or dependency.

Envy and Jealousy: When others express envy or jealousy of the narcissist, it can be a source of narcissistic supply. It confirms their perceived superiority.

The Narcissistic Feedback Loop

Understanding the concept of narcissistic supply helps illuminate the cyclical nature of narcissistic behavior. Narcissists engage in behaviors designed to elicit admiration and validation, creating a feedback loop of needing more supply to sustain their self-image. When their supply is threatened, they may resort to manipulation, control, or aggression to regain it.

Recognizing Narcissistic Supply in Relationships

In personal and professional relationships, recognizing when someone is acting as a source of narcissistic supply is essential. This awareness allows you to set healthy boundaries, maintain your self-esteem, and make informed decisions about whether to engage with the narcissist.

As we delve deeper into this chapter, we will explore strategies for handling narcissistic supply, setting boundaries, and maintaining your well-being when dealing with narcissistic individuals. By understanding the mechanisms at play, you can navigate these complex relationships with greater confidence and resilience.

2.5 Differentiating Between NPD and Other Personality Disorders

Narcissistic Personality Disorder (NPD) shares traits with several other personality disorders, which can make diagnosis and differentiation a challenging task. In this section, we will delve into the intricacies of distinguishing NPD from other personality disorders, shedding light on their unique features and overlaps.

Understanding the Diagnostic Challenge

NPD vs. Borderline Personality Disorder (BPD): Both NPD and BPD can involve intense mood swings and difficulties in maintaining stable relationships. However, while narcissists often present an inflated sense of self-importance, borderlines tend to have a fragile self-identity.

NPD vs. Antisocial Personality Disorder (ASPD): Narcissists and individuals with ASPD can exhibit manipulative behaviors. However, narcissists primarily seek admiration and validation, whereas those with ASPD often engage in exploitative and deceitful actions without the need for admiration.

NPD vs. Histrionic Personality Disorder (HPD): Individuals with HPD often seek attention, similar to narcissists. However, histrionics are more concerned with being the center of attention for the sake of it, while narcissists desire attention that reinforces their grandiose self-image.

NPD vs. Obsessive-Compulsive Personality Disorder (OCPD): Both disorders involve rigid thinking and a preoccupation with control. However, OCPD is more about perfectionism and control over details, while

NPD revolves around the need for admiration and validation.

Key Features of NPD for Differentiation

To differentiate NPD from other personality disorders, consider these key features:

Grandiosity: NPD is characterized by grandiosity, an inflated sense of self-importance, and a constant need for admiration. This core feature distinguishes it from other disorders.

Lack of Empathy: Narcissists often lack empathy and struggle to consider others' feelings or needs, differentiating them from borderline personality, which can involve intense empathy and emotional reactivity.

Manipulation for Validation: The manipulative behavior exhibited by narcissists is mainly aimed at obtaining narcissistic supply, while individuals with ASPD manipulate for personal gain.

Superficial Relationships: Narcissists tend to form superficial, exploitative relationships, as opposed to individuals with histrionic personality disorder, who may genuinely desire close relationships.

Perceived Entitlement: The sense of entitlement in NPD distinguishes it from obsessive-compulsive personality disorder, which focuses on control but not necessarily on feeling entitled to special treatment.

Recognizing these distinctions is crucial for an accurate diagnosis and an effective approach to dealing with individuals with NPD. In the following sections, we will explore strategies for managing and interacting with narcissists based on their specific traits and behaviors.

Chapter 3: The Impact of Narcissism

3.1 Narcissism in Relationships

Narcissism's influence extends far beyond an individual's internal world; it significantly impacts the dynamics of their relationships, whether with family, friends, or romantic partners. In this section, we will explore the profound implications of narcissism on different types of relationships and the challenges it poses.

The Narcissistic Relationship Dynamic

Narcissism, at its core, revolves around self-centeredness, entitlement, and the relentless pursuit of admiration and validation. When this dynamic enters a relationship, whether it's a close friendship or an intimate partnership, it can introduce a myriad of complexities:

Emotional Drain: Being in a relationship with a narcissist can be emotionally exhausting. Their constant need for validation and admiration can drain their partners and leave them feeling emotionally depleted.

Manipulation: Narcissists are skilled manipulators. They may employ tactics like gaslighting, guilt-tripping, and emotional blackmail to maintain control and secure their narcissistic supply.

Shallow Connections: Narcissists often struggle to form deep, meaningful connections. Their relationships tend to be superficial, lacking the emotional intimacy that many people seek in their interactions.

Lack of Empathy: Empathy is a crucial component of healthy relationships. Narcissists, however, often lack the ability to genuinely empathize with others, making it challenging for their partners to feel understood and supported.

Impact on Various Relationships

The influence of narcissism can vary depending on the type of relationship. Here's how it manifests in different contexts:

Family Relationships: Narcissism within families can disrupt harmony, causing tension and emotional strife. Siblings, parents, and children may struggle to navigate the challenges posed by a narcissistic family member.

Friendships: Narcissistic friends may frequently take more than they give, leaving their friends feeling used and unappreciated. Friendships with narcissists can be one-sided and emotionally taxing.

Romantic Partnerships: Being in a romantic relationship with a narcissist can be particularly challenging. The constant need for admiration can lead to instability, emotional abuse, and the erosion of self-esteem.

Workplace Relationships: Narcissistic colleagues or superiors can create a hostile work environment. Their manipulative behavior can undermine teamwork and collaboration.

Coping with Narcissism in Relationships

Understanding the impact of narcissism on relationships is the first step in managing these complex dynamics. In the subsequent sections of this chapter, we will explore strategies and coping mechanisms for dealing with narcissistic individuals in various relationship contexts. These insights will empower you to protect your emotional well-being, set boundaries, and make informed decisions when confronted with narcissism in your personal and professional life.

3.2 Narcissism in the Workplace

Narcissism's far-reaching influence is not confined to personal relationships; it also permeates the professional sphere. In this section, we will delve into the complex dynamics of narcissism in the workplace, how it affects colleagues, teams, and organizations, and strategies for navigating these challenges.

Recognizing Narcissism in the Professional Environment

Identifying narcissism in a workplace context can be essential for maintaining a healthy work environment and individual well-being. Here are some common behaviors and characteristics to watch for:

Grandiose Self-Image: Narcissists in the workplace often exhibit an inflated sense of self-importance. They may believe they are more competent and valuable than their colleagues, making collaboration difficult.

Seeking Constant Admiration: Narcissistic individuals frequently seek admiration and recognition for their contributions. They may demand excessive praise or become hostile when they feel underappreciated.

Manipulative Behavior: Narcissists in the professional setting can employ manipulation tactics to further their agenda. This may include undermining coworkers, taking credit for others' work, and using deceptive strategies to gain favor.

Lack of Empathy: Narcissists tend to prioritize their own needs over the well-being of their colleagues. They may show little empathy or concern for the struggles and challenges faced by their coworkers.

Impact on Colleagues and Teams

The presence of a narcissist in the workplace can have several adverse effects:

Team Disruption: Narcissists often create discord within teams. Their self-centered behavior can undermine collaboration, hinder communication, and lead to conflicts among team members.

Stifled Creativity: The need for control and recognition can stifle creativity and innovative thinking within a group. Team members may become hesitant to share ideas or challenge the narcissist's opinions.

High Turnover: A workplace characterized by narcissistic behavior can experience high turnover rates. Employees may choose to leave due to the toxic environment created by the narcissist.

<u>*Coping with Narcissism in the Workplace*</u>

Effectively dealing with narcissism in a professional setting requires a combination of strategies and self-care. Here are some approaches to consider:

Set Boundaries: Establish clear boundaries to protect yourself from the negative impact of a narcissistic colleague or superior. This may include limiting engagement in their manipulative tactics and seeking support from HR when necessary.

Maintain Professionalism: Responding to narcissistic behavior with professionalism is essential. Avoid engaging in personal conflicts and focus on work-related matters.

Document Interactions: Keeping records of interactions with a narcissistic coworker can be valuable if you need to report inappropriate behavior or discuss the issue with higher management.

Seek Support: Share your experiences with a trusted coworker or supervisor. They may offer guidance or connect you with resources to address the situation.

Self-Care: Ensure that you prioritize self-care and maintain a support network outside of the workplace. Coping with narcissism can be emotionally draining, so it's crucial to safeguard your well-being.

In the following sections of this chapter, we will delve deeper into specific scenarios and provide guidance on handling narcissism in the professional environment, allowing you to navigate these challenging dynamics with greater resilience and confidence.

3.3 The Toll on Family and Friends

The repercussions of narcissism extend far beyond individual relationships or the workplace; they significantly affect the lives of those closest to the narcissist. In this section, we'll explore the profound impact of narcissism on family members and friends, the challenges they face, and strategies for coping with these complex dynamics.

Narcissism often exerts a heavy toll on family relationships. When a family member, such as a parent, spouse, or sibling, exhibits narcissistic traits or has Narcissistic Personality Disorder (NPD), the effects can be emotionally and psychologically taxing. Here are some common challenges faced by family members:

Emotional Manipulation: Narcissistic family members may engage in emotional manipulation to maintain control and elicit attention and admiration. This can lead to a perpetual cycle of emotional turmoil for those around them.

Parenting Challenges: Narcissistic parents may struggle to provide the emotional support and consistency that children need. The children of narcissistic parents may grapple with self-esteem issues, anxiety, and difficulty forming healthy relationships.

Unpredictable Behavior: The inconsistent and unpredictable nature of narcissistic behavior can leave family members walking on eggshells, unsure of how to avoid triggering anger or disappointment.

Impact on Friends and Social Circles

Narcissism also affects friendships and social circles. Friends of narcissists often face unique challenges:

One-Sided Relationships: Friendships with narcissists tend to be one-sided, with the narcissist monopolizing conversations and interactions. Friends may feel unappreciated or used.

Drama and Conflict: Narcissistic friends often introduce drama and conflict into social gatherings. Their need for attention and admiration can lead to uncomfortable situations or disputes.

Emotional Exhaustion: Maintaining a friendship with a narcissist can be emotionally exhausting. Friends may find themselves continually offering emotional support without receiving the same in return.

Coping Strategies for Family and Friends

Dealing with a narcissistic family member or friend necessitates a unique set of coping strategies:

Establish Boundaries: Setting clear boundaries is vital for safeguarding your emotional well-being. Identify behaviors you won't tolerate and communicate these boundaries assertively but calmly.

Seek Professional Help: Family therapy or counseling can provide a safe space for addressing the challenges of dealing with narcissism within the family. A trained therapist can guide the family toward healthier dynamics.

Limit Contact: In some cases, limiting contact with the narcissistic individual may be necessary to protect your mental health. Reducing exposure to their toxic behavior can be a valid form of self-care.

Build a Support Network: Lean on friends and other family members for support. Sharing your experiences with people who understand the situation can help you feel less isolated.

Practice Self-Care: Prioritize self-care by engaging in activities that bring you joy and relaxation. Maintaining your well-being is essential when dealing with the emotional toll of narcissism.

In the subsequent sections of this chapter, we'll delve deeper into specific scenarios and provide guidance for handling the impact of narcissism on family and friends, enabling you to navigate these challenging relationships with resilience and self-compassion.

3.4 Societal and Cultural Aspects

Narcissism is not confined to individual relationships and personal dynamics; it is also deeply intertwined with societal and cultural factors. In this section, we will dissect the broader impact of narcissism on society, cultural trends, and its presence in various domains.

The Culture of Narcissism

In recent decades, there has been a growing concern about what some sociologists and psychologists refer to as "the culture of narcissism." This term describes a societal shift toward values and behaviors that prioritize self-absorption, entitlement, and the pursuit of external validation.

Social Media and the Selfie Culture: The rise of social media platforms has fueled self-presentation and self-promotion. It has become increasingly common for individuals to curate idealized versions of their lives online, seeking validation through likes, comments, and followers. This phenomenon has been closely linked to the amplification of narcissistic traits in society.

Consumerism and Materialism: Consumer culture often encourages the pursuit of material possessions and external markers of success as a source of self-worth. This emphasis on external validation aligns with narcissistic tendencies.

Celebrity and Fame: In contemporary society, fame and celebrity status are often idealized. The allure of fame can feed into narcissistic aspirations and behaviors.

Narcissistic traits can manifest in different aspects of society:

Politics: The political arena is no stranger to narcissism. Narcissistic leaders may prioritize their image and success over the well-being of their constituents, leading to divisive policies and a focus on power and personal gain.

Workplace: Narcissistic traits can be disruptive in the workplace. Employees or leaders with high narcissism may prioritize self-advancement over teamwork and collaboration, which can lead to strained working relationships.

Entertainment and Media: The entertainment industry often celebrates self-promotion and fame. This environment can foster narcissistic behaviors and tendencies, both among entertainers and those pursuing fame.

Advertising and Marketing: Advertisers sometimes employ tactics that appeal to narcissistic desires. These strategies often play on the idea that consumers need certain products to enhance their self-esteem or image.

Coping with Societal and Cultural Narcissism

Understanding and navigating societal and cultural narcissism can be challenging, but it is not insurmountable. Here are some strategies for individuals and communities:

Media Literacy: Developing media literacy skills can help individuals critically evaluate messages in the media and recognize when marketing and advertising play on narcissistic themes.

Promoting Empathy: Encouraging empathy in education and society can help counter the negative effects of narcissistic cultural trends. Empathy fosters a focus on others and the well-being of the community.

Collective Action: Communities and individuals can work together to address societal issues related to narcissism. This may involve advocating for policies that prioritize the common good over individual gain.

Supportive Communities: Building and participating in supportive communities that prioritize authentic connections and values can provide a counterbalance to the isolating aspects of societal narcissism.

The impact of narcissism on society and culture is a multifaceted issue. By understanding these dynamics and taking proactive steps to promote healthy values and behaviors, we can collectively work toward a more balanced and empathetic society.

In the subsequent sections of this chapter, we'll further examine the impact of narcissism in specific contexts, providing insights and strategies to navigate these complex dynamics.

3.5 The Narcissistic Cycle of Abuse

Narcissistic abuse is a devastating and often repetitive pattern of behavior inflicted by those with narcissistic traits or Narcissistic Personality Disorder (NPD). In this section, we will delve into the insidious cycle of narcissistic abuse, providing insight into its phases, the psychological impact on victims, and strategies for breaking free.

Understanding the Narcissistic Cycle of Abuse

The narcissistic cycle of abuse typically consists of three main phases:

1. Idealization: In the initial phase, often referred to as "love-bombing," the narcissist

idealizes the victim. They shower the victim with affection, compliments, and attention, making the victim feel special and loved. This phase is designed to create an intense emotional bond and gain the victim's trust.

2. Devaluation: After the idealization phase, the narcissist's behavior takes a sharp turn. They begin to devalue the victim, using criticism, manipulation, and emotional abuse. The victim's self-esteem is eroded as they are subjected to constant criticism and belittling.

3. Discard or Hoovering: In the final phase, the narcissist may either discard the victim, abruptly ending the relationship, or engage in hoovering—attempting to draw the victim back into the cycle. Hoovering often involves apologies, promises to change, and further manipulation.

Victims of narcissistic abuse often experience a wide range of emotional and psychological consequences, including:

Low Self-Esteem: Constant criticism and devaluation can lead to a profound sense of worthlessness.

Anxiety and Depression: The unpredictable nature of the narcissistic cycle can result in chronic anxiety and depression.

Isolation: Narcissists often isolate their victims from friends and family, making it difficult for them to seek support.

Complex Post-Traumatic Stress Disorder (C-PTSD): Victims may develop symptoms similar to those of post-traumatic stress disorder (PTSD) due to the ongoing abuse.

Escaping the narcissistic cycle of abuse is challenging but essential for healing and recovery. Here are some strategies for those seeking to break free:

No Contact: Whenever possible, maintaining no contact with the narcissist is the most effective way to end the cycle. This may involve blocking communication and avoiding any interaction.

Seeking Support: Victims of narcissistic abuse benefit from the support of therapists, support groups, and trusted friends and family.

Rebuilding Self-Esteem: Rebuilding self-esteem is a crucial part of recovery. This may involve therapy, self-help resources, and self-compassion practices.

Legal Protections: In some cases, legal action, such as restraining orders, may be necessary to protect victims from ongoing abuse.

Empowering Survivors

Survivors of narcissistic abuse can heal, recover, and go on to lead fulfilling lives. This section will explore strategies and resources to help victims escape the narcissistic cycle of abuse, rebuild their lives, and protect themselves from future harm.

In the subsequent sections of this chapter, we'll further examine the impact of narcissism in various contexts and provide guidance on healing and recovery for victims of narcissistic abuse.

Chapter 4: Coping and Self-Care

4.1 Self-Care Strategies for Dealing with a Narcissist

Coping with a narcissist can be emotionally and mentally exhausting. In this section, we'll explore effective self-care strategies that can help you maintain your well-being while navigating a relationship with a narcissist.

Understanding the Importance of Self-Care

Self-care is the practice of deliberately taking time to care for your physical, mental, and emotional health. When dealing with a narcissist, self-care becomes a vital tool for maintaining your resilience and mental clarity.

Establish Boundaries: Setting clear and firm boundaries is essential when dealing with a narcissist. Communicate your boundaries assertively and consistently. Remember that narcissists may push back, but maintaining boundaries is crucial for your well-being.

Self-Awareness: Cultivate self-awareness to recognize the emotional toll of interacting with a narcissist. Pay attention to your emotions and stress levels. Self-awareness is the first step in self-care.

Seek Support: You don't have to go through this alone. Reach out to friends, family, or a therapist who can provide emotional support and guidance. Support groups for individuals dealing with narcissists can also be invaluable.

Practice Stress Reduction Techniques: Stress can be a constant companion when dealing with narcissistic personalities. Engage in stress-reduction techniques such as mindfulness, meditation, yoga, or deep breathing exercises to help manage your stress.

Self-Compassion: Be kind and compassionate to yourself. It's common to blame oneself or feel guilt when dealing with a narcissist's manipulation. Practice self-compassion to counteract these negative feelings.

Limit Contact: In some situations, limiting contact with the narcissist can be a form of self-care. Reducing interactions, particularly when they turn toxic, can help protect your mental health.

Engage in Hobbies: Pursue hobbies and activities that bring you joy and fulfillment. These positive experiences can serve as a counterbalance to the negativity in your interactions with the narcissist.

Educate Yourself: Knowledge is empowering. Learn more about narcissism and narcissistic personality disorder to understand the behavior patterns and manipulation tactics employed by narcissists.

Maintain Physical Health: Ensure you are taking care of your physical health through regular exercise, a balanced diet, and adequate sleep. Physical well-being is closely connected to emotional resilience.

Avoid the Blame Game: Recognize that you cannot change or fix a narcissist. Avoid blaming yourself for their behavior. Focus on what you can control—your reactions and self-care.

Safety Measures: If the situation involves potential physical or emotional danger, have a safety plan in place. This may include knowing when and how to involve law enforcement or seeking a restraining order.

Self-Care Is Your Anchor

Remember that self-care isn't selfish; it's a necessity when dealing with a narcissist. The strategies discussed in this section will help you maintain your emotional well-being, navigate difficult relationships, and ultimately protect yourself from the harmful effects of prolonged exposure to narcissistic behavior.

In the following sections of this chapter, we will further explore coping strategies, emotional resilience, and the journey to healing and recovery for those dealing with narcissistic individuals.

4.2 Setting Boundaries

Setting boundaries is a fundamental aspect of dealing with a narcissist. In this section, we will explore the importance of establishing and maintaining clear boundaries and provide practical guidance on how to do so effectively.

The Importance of Boundaries

1. Protection of Your Well-Being: Boundaries are like a shield that guards your emotional and mental well-being. When dealing with a narcissist, it's crucial to prioritize your own mental health.

2. Defining Acceptable Behavior: Boundaries provide a framework for what you deem as acceptable and unacceptable behavior. This clarity can help minimize confusion and emotional turmoil.

3. Preventing Manipulation: Narcissists are often skilled at manipulation. Boundaries can serve as a barrier against their attempts to control or influence you.

4. Fostering Self-Respect: Setting boundaries is an act of self-respect. It sends the message that you value yourself and your feelings.

Establishing Boundaries with a Narcissist

Identify Your Limits: Self-awareness is the first step. Reflect on your emotional triggers and the behavior that you find unacceptable. What are your limits?

Communicate Clearly: Clearly and assertively communicate your boundaries to the narcissist. Be specific about the behaviors that are problematic, and express your expectations.

Use "I" Statements: When communicating your boundaries, use "I" statements to convey your feelings and needs. For example, "I feel uncomfortable when..." or "I need..."

Be Consistent: Narcissists may test your boundaries. It's crucial to remain consistent in upholding them. Don't waver or make exceptions that compromise your well-being.

Resist Guilt: The narcissist may use guilt or manipulation to persuade you to drop your boundaries. Stay firm and remind yourself of the importance of self-care.

Enforce Consequences: If the narcissist continually crosses your boundaries, you may need to enforce consequences, such as limiting contact or seeking professional help.

Seek Support: Reach out to friends, family, or a therapist who can provide emotional support and guidance as you navigate this challenging process.

The Challenges of Setting Boundaries

Setting boundaries with a narcissist can be challenging. They may resist, become angry, or attempt to undermine your efforts. It's essential to remain resilient and remember that these reactions are a testament to the effectiveness of your boundaries.

In this section, we have explored the importance of setting boundaries when dealing with a narcissist. The next part of this chapter will delve into strategies for emotional resilience and self-care as you continue to navigate complex relationships with narcissistic individuals.

4.3 Maintaining Emotional Health

Maintaining emotional health is paramount when dealing with a narcissist. In this section, we'll delve into strategies and practices that will help you safeguard your emotional well-being as you navigate the complexities of such relationships.

Understanding Emotional Health

1. Self-Awareness: Emotional health begins with self-awareness. Understanding your emotions, triggers, and coping mechanisms is crucial. It empowers you to make informed choices about how you react to a narcissist's behavior.

2. Self-Regulation: Emotional health involves the ability to manage and regulate your emotions. This is especially important when dealing with someone who may try to provoke or manipulate your feelings.

3. Resilience: Resilience is your capacity to bounce back from difficult situations. Building resilience equips you to handle the ups and downs of interacting with a narcissist without being deeply affected.

4. Seeking Support: Emotional health is often reinforced through social support.

Whether from friends, family, or a therapist, having a support system can provide an outlet for expressing and processing your feelings.

Strategies for Maintaining Emotional Health

Practice Mindfulness: Mindfulness techniques, such as meditation and deep breathing exercises, can help you stay grounded and focused during challenging interactions.

Self-Reflection: Regular self-reflection allows you to assess your emotional state. Consider maintaining a journal to record your feelings and experiences.

Boundaries: As discussed earlier, setting and maintaining boundaries are vital for emotional health. They create a protective space that allows you to nurture your emotional well-being.

Emotional Detachment: Learning to emotionally detach from a narcissist's attempts to provoke you is a valuable skill. It involves recognizing their behavior without letting it affect your inner peace.

Self-Care Routine: Develop a self-care routine that addresses your emotional needs. This can include hobbies, exercise, or any activity that brings you joy and relaxation.

Therapy: Consider seeking therapy or counseling. A mental health professional can provide you with tools to manage your emotions and cope with the challenges of dealing with a narcissist.

Dealing with Emotional Manipulation

Narcissists often employ emotional manipulation tactics. Recognizing these strategies is the first step to protecting your emotional health. In the next section, we'll explore common manipulation techniques and how to counteract them.

In this section, we have delved into the importance of maintaining emotional health when dealing with a narcissist. The subsequent part of this chapter will focus on strategies for coping with emotional manipulation and ensuring your well-being remains a top priority.

4.4 Seeking Support

When dealing with a narcissist, seeking support is more than a valuable option; it's often a necessity. This section delves into the importance of seeking support from friends, family, or professionals and how it can significantly impact your journey toward managing a narcissistic relationship.

Validation: Interactions with a narcissist can often leave you questioning your reality. Seeking support from those you trust can validate your experiences and feelings, assuring you that you're not alone.

Emotional Outlet: Friends and family can serve as a safe space for you to express your emotions. Sharing your experiences with those who understand can be cathartic.

Objective Perspective: A trusted confidant can offer an objective view of your situation, helping you see things more clearly. Their insights may help you devise better coping strategies.

Preventing Isolation: Narcissists may attempt to isolate you from your support network. Recognizing this, and maintaining these connections, is essential for your emotional health.

Friends and Family: Those closest to you can provide immediate support. They are often the first line of defense against emotional manipulation.

Support Groups: Many find solace in support groups, whether in person or online. These groups are composed of individuals who share similar experiences, offering empathy and coping strategies.

Therapy or Counseling: Professional help from a therapist or counselor can be incredibly beneficial. They can guide you through the emotional complexities of dealing with a narcissist and help you develop healthy coping mechanisms.

How to Seek Support

Reach Out: Don't hesitate to share your experiences with friends and family you trust. Vulnerability can lead to stronger connections.

Support Groups: Join local or online support groups. These are safe spaces where you can discuss your experiences, gain insights, and provide support to others.

Therapy: Consider therapy or counseling. A mental health professional can offer guidance and support tailored to your unique situation.

Educate Your Support Network: Help your support system understand narcissism and its effects. This will enable them to provide more effective assistance.

Set Boundaries: While seeking support, be mindful of setting boundaries. Ensure your interactions with support networks remain healthy and not overwhelming.

In this section, we've explored the critical role that seeking support plays in your journey of coping and self-care when dealing with a narcissist. The following parts of this chapter will continue to provide you with insights and strategies to navigate this complex terrain.

4.5 Practicing Patience and Empathy

Dealing with a narcissist often requires an abundance of patience and empathy. In this section, we will explore the significance of these qualities and how they can be harnessed as powerful tools in managing a relationship with a narcissist.

Understanding Patience and Empathy

Patience in Action: Patience is not passive resignation but a conscious choice to remain calm and composed in the face of narcissistic behavior. It allows you to avoid immediate emotional reactions and instead respond thoughtfully.

Empathy as a Bridge: Empathy involves understanding and sharing the feelings of another. While it may be challenging to empathize with a narcissist's behavior, developing empathy can help you navigate the relationship more effectively.

The Role of Patience and Empathy

Conflict De-Escalation: When you encounter narcissistic rage or manipulation, responding with patience can help de-escalate conflicts. Rather than fueling the fire, it allows you to maintain control.

Improved Communication: Practicing patience and empathy can lead to more constructive and less confrontational communication with the narcissist, potentially fostering better understanding.

Protecting Your Emotional Well-being: By approaching the situation with patience and empathy, you're less likely to internalize the narcissist's negative behavior, which can protect your emotional health.

Caveats and Limits

Boundaries: It's crucial to maintain healthy boundaries while practicing patience and empathy. These qualities shouldn't be used as an excuse for allowing abuse or manipulation.

Self-Care: Balancing patience and empathy with self-care is essential. Overextending these qualities can lead to emotional exhaustion. Know when to step back for your well-being.

Practical Strategies

Active Listening: Practice active listening skills to better understand the narcissist's perspective, even if you don't agree. This can defuse tension and lead to more productive conversations.

Refocus on Yourself: Regularly remind yourself of your own needs and boundaries. Don't sacrifice your well-being for the sake of patience and empathy.

Seeking Professional Guidance: In complex situations, involving a therapist or counselor can help you hone your patience and empathy and provide a safe space to process your experiences.

The Balance of Self-Care

Remember that practicing patience and empathy doesn't mean tolerating abuse or manipulation. Striking a balance between these qualities and self-care is key to successfully navigating a relationship with a narcissist.

In the following sections of this chapter, we will explore further coping strategies and self-care techniques to help you manage the challenges that come with dealing with a narcissist.

Chapter 5: Strategies for Managing a Narcissist

5.1 Communication Techniques

Effective communication with a narcissist can be a challenging yet essential aspect of managing the relationship. In this section, we'll explore various communication techniques that can help you navigate conversations and interactions with a narcissist while minimizing conflicts and emotional turmoil.

The Art of Communication

Active Listening: Engage in active listening to demonstrate that you value their perspective, even if you don't agree. This can reduce defensiveness and lead to more constructive dialogues.

Use "I" Statements: Frame your statements using "I" instead of "You." For example, say,

"I feel hurt when..." instead of "You always hurt me when..." This helps prevent the narcissist from feeling attacked.

Avoid Accusations: Refrain from making accusatory statements. Focus on expressing your feelings and needs without blaming the narcissist.

Stay Calm: Maintain a composed demeanor during conversations, even if the narcissist becomes agitated. Your calmness can have a soothing effect and prevent escalation.

Setting Clear Boundaries

Establish Boundaries: Clearly define your boundaries and communicate them to the narcissist. Be firm and consistent in upholding these boundaries.

Consequences: Communicate the consequences for crossing your boundaries. This can serve as a deterrent for inappropriate behavior.

Stick to Your Boundaries: The key to boundary setting is consistency. Be prepared to enforce your boundaries and follow through with consequences when necessary.

Strategic Timing

Choose the Right Time: Pick an appropriate time for discussions. Avoid bringing up sensitive topics during arguments or when the narcissist is particularly agitated.

Stay Focused: Keep conversations focused on the issue at hand. Narcissists can be skilled at deflecting blame, so gently steer the conversation back to the topic.

Dealing with Manipulation

Recognize Manipulation: Be aware of manipulation tactics such as gaslighting, guilt-tripping, and blame-shifting. If you notice these behaviors, address them calmly and directly.

Detoxify Conversations: When you sense that a conversation is becoming manipulative or emotionally charged, take a step back and revisit it when emotions have cooled.

Support and Professional Guidance

Seek Support: Don't hesitate to reach out to trusted friends, family, or support groups. Discussing your experiences can provide emotional relief and different perspectives.

Therapeutic Intervention: Consider involving a therapist or counselor in your communication efforts. A neutral third party can facilitate productive dialogues.

Remember that effective communication with a narcissist is an ongoing process. It may not yield immediate results, but over time, employing these techniques can help you navigate interactions with more confidence and less emotional turmoil.

In the subsequent sections of this chapter, we will explore further strategies for managing a narcissist, including ways to protect your emotional well-being and establish a sense of control within the relationship.

5.2 Dealing with Manipulation

Manipulation is a hallmark of narcissistic behavior, and understanding how to effectively deal with it is a crucial skill when managing a relationship with a narcissist. In this section, we will delve into strategies for recognizing and addressing manipulation.

Recognizing Manipulation

Identifying Gaslighting: Gaslighting is a common manipulation tactic used by narcissists. It involves the narcissist attempting to distort your reality, making you question your perception of events.

Recognize when this occurs by paying attention to inconsistencies and trust your instincts.

Spotting Guilt-Tripping: Narcissists often employ guilt-tripping as a means of control. They may try to make you feel responsible for their emotions or actions. Acknowledge these attempts, and remember that you are not responsible for their feelings.

Addressing Blame-Shifting: When the narcissist shifts blame for their actions onto you or others, it's essential to confront this manipulation. Stay focused on the facts and assert your boundaries.

Responding to Manipulation

Stay Calm: When you recognize manipulation, the narcissist may escalate their efforts. It's crucial to remain calm. Emotions can cloud your judgment, so keep a clear mind during these interactions.

Question with Confidence: If you suspect manipulation, don't be afraid to ask questions for clarification. Narcissists often struggle with providing straightforward answers.

Set Firm Boundaries: Reiterate your boundaries and your expectations for respectful communication. Be consistent in upholding these boundaries, especially when faced with manipulation.

Seek Neutral Ground: If you're unable to engage in a productive conversation because of manipulation, suggest involving a therapist or counselor as a neutral mediator.

Detoxifying Manipulative Conversations

Take a Break: If a conversation becomes manipulative or emotionally charged, it can be beneficial to step away and revisit it when both parties are calmer and more composed.

Record Conversations: If manipulation is persistent and you're met with denial, consider keeping records of your interactions. This can help you maintain clarity and objectivity.

Seeking Professional Help

Therapeutic Intervention: Consider involving a therapist or counselor experienced in narcissism and personality disorders. A neutral third party can guide conversations and facilitate understanding.

Support Systems: Engage with a support network, which can provide emotional relief and insights into coping with manipulation.

Dealing with manipulation from a narcissist is a challenging aspect of managing such relationships. By recognizing manipulation tactics, staying calm, setting boundaries, and seeking support, you can navigate these situations with increased confidence and emotional well-being. In the upcoming sections of this chapter, we will explore more strategies for managing a narcissist, enhancing your ability to maintain a sense of control and personal growth within the relationship.

5.3 Conflict Resolution

Conflict is an inevitable part of any relationship, and when dealing with a narcissist, it's essential to approach conflicts with a thoughtful and strategic mindset. In this section, we will explore conflict resolution techniques tailored to managing a narcissistic individual.

Understanding Conflict Dynamics

Narcissistic Reactions: Recognize that conflicts with narcissists can trigger intense reactions. They may become defensive, aggressive, or engage in blame-shifting. Understanding these patterns can help you navigate the conflict more effectively.

Avoid Power Struggles: Narcissists often crave control and dominance. Avoid engaging in power struggles, as it can escalate the situation. Instead, aim for collaboration and problem-solving.

Conflict Resolution Strategies

Stay Calm and Collected: Maintaining emotional composure during a conflict is crucial. Narcissists may attempt to provoke emotional reactions, so your calm demeanor can be a powerful tool.

Active Listening: Narcissists appreciate being heard. Practice active listening by acknowledging their concerns and repeating their points. This can help de-escalate tensions.

Use "I" Statements: When expressing your feelings and needs, use "I" statements to avoid sounding accusatory. For example, say, "I feel hurt when..." instead of "You always..."

Set Clear Objectives: Clearly define the issue at hand and your desired outcome. Narcissists may use diversions or deflection to avoid addressing the real problem. Keep the conversation on track.

Avoid Personal Attacks: Stick to the specific issue at hand and avoid personal attacks or criticisms. Be constructive in your feedback.

Stay Solution-Oriented: Shift the focus from blame to finding a solution. Emphasize that you both have a shared interest in resolving the conflict.

Boundaries and Compromise

Reiterate Boundaries: In the midst of conflict, reaffirm your boundaries and expectations for respectful behavior. Narcissists may test boundaries, but consistency is key.

Know When to Compromise: Recognize that not all conflicts can be resolved in your favor. Choose your battles and be willing to compromise when it doesn't compromise your well-being.

When to Seek External Mediation

Therapeutic Intervention: In some cases, the involvement of a therapist or counselor may be necessary to mediate conflicts. They can provide a neutral environment and professional guidance.

Support Systems: Lean on your support network, such as friends and family, for advice and emotional support during and after conflicts.

Conflict resolution with a narcissist requires patience and tact. By understanding the dynamics of conflict in such relationships, practicing effective communication, maintaining boundaries, and knowing when to seek external mediation, you can navigate these challenging situations with more confidence and resilience. In the following sections of this chapter, we will explore additional strategies for effectively managing a narcissist and maintaining your well-being within the relationship.

5.4 Grey Rock Method

Dealing with a narcissist often necessitates creative approaches to protect your emotional well-being and maintain your boundaries. The Grey Rock Method is one such strategy that can be particularly effective.

Understanding the Grey Rock Method

The Grey Rock Method is a technique designed to make yourself as uninteresting and unreactive as a grey rock. By doing so, you reduce the narcissist's interest in manipulating or engaging with you emotionally. This method is especially useful when you cannot entirely cut off contact with the narcissist, such as in shared custody situations, at work, or with family members.

Implementing the Grey Rock Method

Emotional Detachment: The core of the Grey Rock Method is emotional detachment. Limit emotional reactions, both positive and negative, when interacting with the narcissist. Keep your emotions neutral.

Minimal Engagement: Converse with the narcissist only when necessary, and keep your conversations brief and to the point. Avoid providing personal information or emotional responses.

Bland and Uninteresting: Present yourself as unexciting and unremarkable. Share mundane, non-provocative details about your life to discourage further inquiry.

Avoid Jargon: Steer clear of using jargon or emotional language. Keep your communication simple and unemotional.

Focus on Practical Matters: When conversations are unavoidable, stick to practical matters or topics unrelated to your personal life. Redirect the discussion to neutral subjects.

Consistency: Maintain consistency in your behavior. The narcissist may try to provoke reactions by being provocative or charming. Stay steady in your approach.

The Benefits of the Grey Rock Method

The Grey Rock Method can yield several advantages in managing interactions with a narcissist:

Emotional Protection: By detaching emotionally and minimizing reactions, you shield yourself from the emotional manipulation the narcissist often employs.

Reduced Supply: Narcissists thrive on emotional reactions and attention. The Grey Rock Method limits their ability to extract narcissistic supply from you.

Maintained Boundaries: This technique helps in enforcing and maintaining personal boundaries, ensuring that you don't divulge personal information or engage in conflicts.

Minimized Stress: Dealing with a narcissist can be mentally and emotionally draining. The Grey Rock Method can reduce the stress and emotional turmoil associated with these interactions.

Challenges and Considerations

While the Grey Rock Method can be effective, it's essential to be aware of potential challenges:

Persistence: Narcissists may escalate their efforts to elicit reactions when they sense your emotional detachment. Staying consistent with the Grey Rock Method is crucial.

Safety: If you believe that implementing this method might put you at risk of harm or retaliation, consider other strategies and seek support from professionals or authorities as needed.

The Grey Rock Method is a valuable tool for managing interactions with a narcissist, especially when disengagement is not an option. By maintaining emotional detachment and minimizing engagement, you can navigate these encounters while safeguarding your emotional well-being. In the subsequent sections of this chapter, we'll delve further into strategies and techniques for effectively managing a relationship with a narcissist.

5.5 Using the "Broken Record" Approach

Effectively managing a relationship with a narcissist often requires a toolkit of strategies. One such technique that can prove highly useful is the "Broken Record" approach. This approach allows you to maintain your boundaries and assert your needs calmly and consistently, even in the face of resistance or manipulation.

Understanding the "Broken Record" Approach

The "Broken Record" technique involves repeating a simple, assertive statement or request in response to a narcissist's attempts to deflect, manipulate, or push your boundaries. The goal is to maintain focus on your message and ensure that your needs are heard and respected.

Clarity and Calmness: Begin by stating your position clearly and calmly. Avoid becoming emotional or argumentative.

Repeat, Don't Explain: When faced with resistance or manipulation, refrain from providing lengthy explanations or engaging in emotional discussions. Instead, politely but firmly repeat your statement.

Stay on Message: Keep your responses focused on your original statement. The narcissist may attempt to divert the conversation, but you should persist in repeating your key message.

Avoid Emotional Triggers: The "Broken Record" approach works best when you remain unemotional and don't take the narcissist's bait. Maintain your composure and consistency.

Assert Boundaries: Use this technique to reinforce your boundaries, whether they relate to personal space, emotional well-being, or expectations of respectful communication.

Benefits of the "Broken Record" Approach

Utilizing the "Broken Record" approach offers several advantages when dealing with narcissistic individuals:

Consistent Messaging: It ensures that your message remains clear and unwavering despite attempts to manipulate or confuse.

Boundary Enforcement: This technique is valuable for enforcing and maintaining your boundaries.

Reduced Emotional Engagement: By sticking to a concise statement and avoiding emotional entanglement, you protect your emotional well-being.

Assertive Communication: The "Broken Record" approach empowers you to communicate assertively, even in challenging interactions.

Decreased Manipulation: Narcissists often thrive on emotional reactions and confusion. The "Broken Record" approach reduces their ability to manipulate you.

Challenges and Considerations

While the "Broken Record" approach is effective, it's essential to consider a few factors:

Persistence: Narcissists may escalate their attempts to divert the conversation or elicit emotional reactions. Staying consistent is key.

Safety: Always prioritize your safety and well-being. If a situation escalates to a point where you feel unsafe, disengage and seek help as necessary.

In the upcoming sections of this chapter, we'll explore additional strategies and techniques to help you manage a relationship with a narcissist successfully. Whether it's in personal relationships, the workplace, or within your family, these strategies empower you to navigate challenging interactions while protecting your emotional health.

Chapter 6: Navigating Relationships

6.1 Romantic Partners

Navigating a romantic relationship with a narcissist can be a particularly challenging journey. It often presents unique complexities that demand careful consideration and the application of effective strategies. In this section, we delve into the dynamics of romantic relationships with narcissistic individuals and explore ways to manage these connections.

The Complexities of Romantic Relationships with Narcissists

Romantic partnerships are a significant part of our lives, filled with emotional highs and lows. However, when a narcissist is involved, the relationship dynamics can become more intricate. Understanding these complexities is the first step in managing and, if necessary, extricating yourself from the situation.

Characteristics of Narcissistic Romantic Partners

Narcissistic romantic partners typically exhibit several common traits, including:

Charming Yet Manipulative: Narcissists are often charming and charismatic, which can be what draws you to them initially. However, this charm can mask manipulative behaviors and a lack of empathy.

Constant Need for Validation: They require constant validation and admiration, which may lead to a disproportionate focus on their needs and desires.

Emotionally Draining: Maintaining a relationship with a narcissist can be emotionally draining. They may create drama and crises to maintain your attention.

Lack of Empathy: Narcissists often struggle to empathize with their partner's feelings and needs. They may dismiss or minimize your emotions.

Control Issues: Narcissistic partners may seek to control your actions, decisions, and social interactions, creating a sense of dependency.

Managing a Romantic Relationship with a Narcissist

If you find yourself in a romantic relationship with a narcissist, it's important to remember that you have choices. While every situation is unique, here are some strategies to consider:

Self-Care: Prioritize self-care. Ensure that you maintain your emotional and mental well-being. Seek support from friends, family, or a therapist.

Set Boundaries: Establish clear boundaries in your relationship. Communicate your needs and expectations assertively.

Seek Professional Help: If the relationship is causing you significant distress, consider couples therapy or individual counseling. A therapist can help you navigate complex emotional dynamics.

Consider Your Long-Term Goals: Reflect on your long-term goals and values. Assess whether the relationship aligns with them. Sometimes, it's necessary to consider a future without the narcissistic partner.

Safety First: If your safety is ever a concern, do not hesitate to reach out to local authorities or support organizations that can help you safely exit the relationship.

Know Your Worth: Remember your worth. A narcissistic partner may undermine your self-esteem, but it's crucial to recognize your value and potential.

Moving Forward

Navigating a romantic relationship with a narcissist is undoubtedly challenging. However, it's important to remember that you have the capacity to make decisions that serve your well-being. This chapter explores the complexities of such relationships and provides strategies for managing them, always keeping your emotional health in focus. In the following sections, we'll delve into the impact of narcissism on other types of relationships, offering guidance to help you navigate these intricate dynamics. Whether it's a familial relationship or a friendship, understanding and managing narcissism is key to maintaining your emotional health and well-being.

6.2 Family Members

Family dynamics are an essential part of our lives, but when narcissism is present among family members, it can create significant challenges. In this section, we delve into the complexities of dealing with narcissistic family members and provide guidance on how to navigate these intricate relationships.

Understanding Narcissism in the Family

Narcissism within a family can manifest in various ways, making it essential to recognize the signs and understand the dynamics. Here's a closer look at the impact of narcissism on familial relationships:

The Scapegoat and Golden Child: In narcissistic family systems, roles are often assigned. The scapegoat may be blamed for family issues and criticized relentlessly, while the golden child is the favored one who can do no wrong. Understanding these roles helps in navigating the family dynamic.

Toxic Family Systems: Narcissistic family systems often create a toxic environment characterized by manipulation, emotional abuse, and a lack of empathy. The family members may feel compelled to cater to the narcissist's needs at the expense of their own well-being.

The Impact on Children: Growing up with a narcissistic parent can have long-lasting effects on a child's self-esteem and emotional health. Understanding these impacts is essential to breaking the cycle of narcissism in the family.

Managing Narcissistic Family Relationships

When dealing with narcissistic family members, setting boundaries and maintaining your emotional well-being are crucial. Here are some strategies to consider:

Boundaries: Set clear and firm boundaries with narcissistic family members. Communicate your limits assertively.

Support System: Build a support system outside of the family. Friends, therapists, or support groups can provide emotional assistance.

Self-Care: Prioritize self-care to manage the emotional toll of a narcissistic family. This includes stress reduction, regular exercise, and seeking professional help if necessary.

Detachment: In some cases, detachment may be necessary for self-preservation. This doesn't necessarily mean cutting off contact but reducing emotional involvement.

Seeking Professional Help: If the family dynamic is causing significant distress, consider family therapy or individual counseling for yourself or other family members.

Breaking the Cycle

Recognizing narcissism within the family and taking steps to manage these relationships is essential for breaking the cycle and preserving your well-being. In the following sections, we'll explore the impact of narcissism in other areas, including friendships and the workplace, providing guidance on how to navigate these intricate dynamics. Remember that, regardless of the complexity of the family relationship, you have the capacity to make choices that prioritize your emotional health and happiness.**

6.3 Friends and Acquaintances

Friendships and social connections are significant aspects of our lives, contributing to our emotional well-being and personal growth. In this section, we explore the complexities of maintaining relationships with narcissistic friends and acquaintances and offer guidance on how to navigate these interactions.

Identifying Narcissism in Friendships

Narcissistic traits can surface within friendships and social circles, often leading to challenging and toxic dynamics. Here are some key points to consider when dealing with narcissistic friends and acquaintances:

Manipulative Behavior: Narcissistic friends may engage in manipulative tactics to maintain control over the friendship or extract admiration and attention. This can lead to a one-sided and emotionally draining relationship.

Boundary Violations: Narcissistic individuals may have a tendency to disregard personal boundaries, making it crucial to establish and maintain these boundaries clearly.

Self-Centeredness: Narcissistic friends may consistently prioritize their needs, often leaving little room for your concerns or well-being. This can be emotionally exhausting.

Narcissistic Supply: In friendships, you might become a source of narcissistic supply, providing admiration and validation. Recognizing this role is the first step toward creating healthier dynamics.

Navigating Narcissistic Friendships

Dealing with narcissistic friends or acquaintances can be challenging, but it's possible to maintain these relationships with a strategic and empathetic approach. Here are some strategies to consider:

Setting Boundaries: Clearly communicate your boundaries and expectations within the friendship. Let your friend know what behavior is acceptable and what is not.

Practice Empathy: Try to understand your friend's perspective and their insecurities that might be driving their narcissistic behavior. This doesn't mean condoning their actions but can help you approach the relationship with empathy.

Manage Your Expectations: Be realistic about what you can expect from the friendship. Understand that your friend may not change, and you'll need to adapt accordingly.

Seek Support: Talk to other friends, family members, or a therapist about your experiences. A support system can provide emotional relief and guidance.

Evaluate the Friendship: At some point, you may need to assess whether the friendship is worth maintaining. If it's causing significant distress and outweighs the benefits, it might be best to reconsider the relationship.

Self-Care: Prioritize self-care strategies to maintain your emotional well-being while dealing with a narcissistic friend. This includes stress reduction, engaging in hobbies, and nurturing other relationships.

Remember, managing narcissistic friendships requires patience and resilience. It's essential to strike a balance between empathetic understanding and self-care to protect your emotional health. In the following sections, we'll explore additional strategies for managing narcissistic behaviors in various aspects of life, including the workplace and romantic relationships.**

6.4 Co-Parenting with a Narcissist

Co-parenting with a narcissist can be one of the most challenging and emotionally draining experiences. It's a situation where the welfare of your children is at stake, and the need for effective strategies to manage this relationship is paramount.

Understanding the Dynamics

Co-parenting with a narcissist often involves navigating a minefield of power struggles, manipulation, and emotional volatility. These are some common traits and behaviors to recognize when co-parenting with a narcissist:

High Conflict: Narcissists thrive on conflict and may provoke disagreements to maintain control or assert dominance.

Unpredictability: Their behavior can be erratic and unpredictable, making it challenging to anticipate their actions or reactions.

Manipulation: Narcissists may use manipulation tactics to undermine your parenting authority and create confusion for the children.

Lack of Empathy: They might prioritize their needs and desires over the children's well-being, showing little empathy for their emotional needs.

Strategies for Effective Co-Parenting

Co-parenting with a narcissist requires a delicate balance of protecting your children's emotional well-being while managing the challenges that come with the co-parent's narcissistic traits. Here are some strategies for effective co-parenting:

Establish Clear Boundaries: Define and communicate boundaries with your co-parent. It's essential to clarify your respective roles and responsibilities regarding the children.

Parallel Parenting: In situations of high conflict, parallel parenting can be more effective than attempting to co-parent. This approach involves minimizing direct communication and interaction, reducing the opportunity for conflict.

Use Written Communication: Communicate with your co-parent in writing whenever possible. This can serve as documentation and reduce the risk of verbal disputes.

Focus on the Children: Keep your focus on your children's best interests. Make decisions based on what is right for them, not what satisfies your co-parent's ego.

Seek Mediation or Legal Assistance: If the situation becomes unmanageable, consider involving a mediator or, if necessary, consult your attorney. Legal support can help enforce boundaries and ensure your children's welfare.

Provide Consistency: Ensure that your children experience a stable and consistent environment between both households. This helps mitigate the emotional turmoil created by the narcissistic co-parent.

Emphasize Emotional Resilience: Teach your children emotional resilience and coping strategies to deal with the challenges they may face when interacting with the narcissistic co-parent.

Self-Care: Maintain your own emotional and mental well-being. Co-parenting with a narcissist can be emotionally exhausting, so prioritize self-care strategies to stay resilient.

Co-parenting with a narcissist is undoubtedly a difficult journey. The focus must always remain on protecting your children and ensuring their emotional and psychological stability. This chapter provides guidance and support for parents dealing with these complex dynamics. The following sections will delve into strategies for navigating other types of relationships affected by narcissistic behaviors.

Chapter 7: In the Workplace

7.1 Recognizing Narcissism in the Office

The prevalence of narcissism in the workplace is a topic of increasing concern. Understanding the signs and symptoms of narcissistic behavior in the professional environment is crucial for both personal well-being and career success. In this section, we will explore how to recognize narcissism in the office.

Identifying Narcissistic Traits

Narcissism in the workplace can manifest in various ways. Recognizing these traits and behaviors is the first step in effectively managing interactions with narcissistic colleagues or superiors. Here are some key traits to watch for:

Grandiosity: Narcissists often exhibit a sense of superiority and entitlement. They may believe they are more knowledgeable or deserving of praise and promotions.

Lack of Empathy: Empathy is typically low in individuals with narcissistic tendencies. They may disregard the feelings and perspectives of coworkers.

Need for Admiration: Narcissists seek constant validation and admiration. They require praise and attention to fuel their ego.

Manipulation: In the workplace, narcissists may use manipulation to advance their interests. This can include playing office politics, undermining colleagues, or taking credit for others' work.

Intolerance of Criticism: Narcissists have a low tolerance for criticism and often react negatively to feedback or constructive suggestions.

Observing Narcissistic Behavior

Recognizing narcissistic behavior is a skill that can be honed over time. Here's how to observe and identify narcissism in the office:

Pay Attention to Conversation Dominance: Narcissists often dominate conversations, steering discussions toward themselves or their achievements.

Notice a Lack of Accountability: When things go wrong, narcissistic individuals may blame others or external factors, avoiding responsibility for their mistakes.

Watch for Boundary Violations: Narcissists may have poor boundaries and encroach on your personal space or time.

Observe Unpredictable Mood Shifts: They can be charming one moment and irritable or hostile the next.

Document Credit-Stealing: Keep records of instances where they take credit for others' work, as this can impact promotions and recognition.

Dealing with Narcissism in the Workplace

Dealing with narcissism in a professional setting can be challenging. However, recognizing narcissistic behavior is the first step in effective management. Subsequent sections in this chapter will explore strategies for navigating the complexities of working with narcissistic colleagues and superiors. Understanding the nature of narcissism can help you protect your well-being, foster healthier workplace dynamics, and ultimately thrive in your career.

7.2 Dealing with a Narcissistic Boss

Navigating a workplace with a narcissistic boss can be particularly challenging. The influence of a narcissistic superior can impact your job satisfaction, emotional well-being, and professional growth. In this section, we'll delve into strategies for effectively dealing with a narcissistic boss.

Understanding the Narcissistic Boss

Working under a narcissistic boss can be emotionally taxing. Understanding their behavior is the first step in developing effective coping strategies:

Recognize Their Insecurities: Narcissistic bosses often hide deep insecurities behind their grandiose facade. Their need for admiration and control may stem from self-doubt.

Ego-Centric Decision-Making: They tend to make decisions based on personal gain or the need for validation, rather than what's best for the team or the organization.

Manipulative Tactics: Narcissistic bosses may use manipulation to maintain their image, such as taking credit for their subordinates' work.

Emotional Roller Coaster: Working with a narcissistic boss can feel like a roller coaster, with unpredictable mood swings and reactions.

Strategies for Managing a Narcissistic Boss

Stay Professional: Maintain professionalism and keep your emotions in check when dealing with a narcissistic boss. Focus on the task at hand rather than personal dynamics.

Clear Communication: Clearly and concisely communicate your ideas and achievements. Narcissistic bosses appreciate directness.

Document Your Contributions: Keep a record of your accomplishments. This can help protect your work from being unjustly claimed by your boss.

Set Boundaries: Establish clear boundaries and expectations for your role. Politely but firmly communicate what you can and cannot do.

Seek Support: Lean on coworkers or mentors for emotional support and guidance. Discussing your experiences with others can help alleviate stress.

Choose Your Battles: Decide when it's worth challenging your boss's behavior. Not every battle is worth fighting, so select your conflicts carefully.

Self-Care: Prioritize self-care to manage the emotional strain of working under a narcissistic boss. This includes stress-reduction techniques, exercise, and maintaining a life outside of work.

Employing Patience and Resilience

Dealing with a narcissistic boss is undoubtedly challenging. Patience and resilience are your allies. By understanding their behavior, staying professional, and implementing effective coping strategies, you can navigate the complexities of the workplace and protect your emotional well-being.

In the subsequent sections of this chapter, we will explore more workplace scenarios, including interactions with narcissistic colleagues and strategies for conflict resolution in a narcissistic work environment.

7.3 Managing Narcissistic Colleagues

Working alongside narcissistic colleagues can present unique challenges in a professional setting. This section explores effective strategies for managing and collaborating with coworkers who exhibit narcissistic traits.

Identifying Narcissistic Colleagues

Before implementing strategies to manage narcissistic colleagues, it's essential to recognize common traits and behaviors:

Self-Centeredness: Narcissistic colleagues tend to be overly self-centered, often diverting conversations and attention to themselves.

Lack of Empathy: They may struggle to empathize with others' feelings and perspectives, making teamwork and cooperation difficult.

Competitiveness: A narcissistic colleague may view coworkers as competition rather than collaborators, leading to office politics and undermining teamwork.

Credit-Seeking Behavior: They might habitually take credit for collective achievements or undermine colleagues to enhance their own image.

Strategies for Managing Narcissistic Colleagues

Maintain Professionalism: When interacting with narcissistic colleagues, remain professional and focused on your tasks and objectives. Avoid being drawn into personal conflicts.

Assertive Communication: Practice assertive communication by clearly expressing your ideas, opinions, and boundaries. Narcissistic colleagues may respect directness.

Document Contributions: Keep records of your work and contributions. This documentation can be useful if you need to demonstrate your achievements in the face of credit-seeking colleagues.

Collaborate Carefully: When necessary, collaborate with caution. Choose your projects and partnerships carefully to minimize potential conflicts.

Seek Mediation: If conflicts escalate, consider involving a supervisor or HR department to mediate and address workplace issues.

Supportive Networks: Build relationships with other colleagues who share your concerns about the narcissistic coworker. A supportive network can provide emotional backing and strategies for managing the situation.

Self-Care: To maintain emotional well-being, prioritize self-care. This includes relaxation techniques, stress management, and finding a healthy work-life balance.

Collaboration with narcissistic colleagues often requires a delicate balance between cooperation and personal boundaries. It's essential to maintain your professionalism, assertive communication, and documentation of contributions. By doing so, you can navigate workplace challenges while preserving your own well-being.

In the following sections of this chapter, we'll delve into strategies for managing conflicts with narcissistic colleagues and explore ways to maintain positive working relationships in a challenging work environment.

7.4 Narcissism and Leadership

This section addresses the complex dynamics of narcissistic individuals in leadership positions within the workplace. It explores how their traits can impact teams and offers guidance on coping with narcissistic bosses and superiors.

Recognizing Narcissistic Leadership

Narcissistic traits in leadership can manifest in various ways:

Charisma and Manipulation: Narcissistic leaders may use charm and charisma to manipulate and gain followers.

Lack of Empathy: They often prioritize their own success over the well-being of their team, demonstrating a lack of empathy.

Micromanagement: Narcissistic leaders may excessively control and micromanage their subordinates, limiting autonomy and creativity.

Credit-Hogging: They might take credit for team accomplishments and deflect blame onto others for failures.

Toxic Competition: A narcissistic leader may foster a competitive, cutthroat atmosphere within the team.

Coping with Narcissistic Leaders

Understanding Their Motivations: Recognizing that a narcissistic leader's actions are primarily driven by self-interest can help you better navigate their decisions.

Documentation: Maintain a record of your contributions, accomplishments, and any interactions with the narcissistic leader, as this can be useful when clarifying your role in projects.

Effective Communication: When communicating with a narcissistic leader, focus on facts and data to support your points. Be concise, clear, and goal-oriented.

Setting Boundaries: Establish clear boundaries within your working relationship. Politely but firmly communicate your limits.

Build Alliances: Connect with colleagues who share your concerns about the leader. Strength in numbers can provide emotional support and a unified approach to addressing workplace issues.

Seek Superiors or HR Intervention: If the situation becomes unbearable, consider discussing the issues with higher management or the human resources department. They may be able to mediate or offer solutions.

The Impact on Teams

Narcissistic leaders can significantly affect their teams. It's essential to be aware of the potential consequences:

Diminished Morale: Team members may experience lower morale due to a lack of recognition and appreciation.

Increased Turnover: Constant turmoil under a narcissistic leader may lead to higher turnover rates, affecting team stability.

Communication Breakdown: The lack of effective communication and collaboration can hinder productivity and innovation.

Burnout: Team members might experience burnout from dealing with a demanding and unsupportive leader.

Maintaining Resilience

Coping with a narcissistic leader requires resilience. It's vital to protect your own well-being by focusing on self-care, building supportive networks, and maintaining a professional demeanor.

In the next section of this chapter, we'll explore strategies for managing relationships with narcissistic colleagues, friends, and acquaintances, providing you with a comprehensive toolkit for navigating these challenging dynamics in the workplace.

Chapter 8: The Recovery Journey

8.1 Leaving or Detaching from a Narcissist

Making the decision to leave or detach from a narcissistic individual is a significant and often challenging step in the journey to recovery. This section offers guidance on recognizing when it's time to disengage from a narcissist and how to navigate this process.

Recognizing the Need to Leave

Unmanageable Abuse: When the narcissistic behavior becomes abusive, physically, emotionally, or psychologically, it is a clear sign that leaving is essential for your safety and well-being.

Repeated Broken Promises: If the narcissist consistently makes empty promises, showing no intention of change, it's an indication that they may not be capable of meaningful transformation.

Loss of Identity: When your sense of self has been eroded by the narcissistic individual, and you find it increasingly challenging to maintain your autonomy and independence.

Recovery Stalled: If your own recovery and personal growth efforts are consistently hindered by the relationship, it may be time to consider moving on.

Planning Your Departure

Secure Your Finances: Ensure that you have financial stability to support yourself after leaving. This might involve saving money or seeking legal advice regarding assets.

Safety Precautions: If you're in an abusive situation, make a safety plan. Identify safe spaces and people who can help during the transition.

Support System: Build a support network of friends and family who can provide emotional support during and after the separation.

Legal Counsel: In cases involving marriage, children, or shared assets, consult with a lawyer to understand your rights and obligations.

Therapeutic Guidance: Consider seeking therapy to help you navigate the emotional challenges of leaving a narcissist.

Detaching Emotionally

Reclaiming Independence: Start rebuilding your sense of self and independence. Focus on your interests, goals, and self-care.

Establish Boundaries: Maintain strict boundaries with the narcissistic individual. Limit contact and avoid engaging in power struggles.

No Contact or Low Contact: Depending on the situation, you may decide to go no contact (completely sever ties) or low contact (minimize communication to essentials).

Healing and Self-Care: Invest time in healing, self-care, and rebuilding your life. This may involve therapy, support groups, and engaging in activities that bring you joy.

Seeking Professional Help

If the process of leaving or detaching becomes emotionally overwhelming or challenging, don't hesitate to seek professional help. Therapists and counselors experienced in dealing with narcissistic abuse can provide guidance and support tailored to your unique situation.

In the next sections of this chapter, we'll delve into the various facets of the recovery journey, offering insights into rebuilding your life and healing from the effects of narcissistic relationships.

8.2 Healing and Self-Discovery

The journey to recovery from a narcissistic relationship involves profound healing and an opportunity for self-discovery. This chapter explores the steps and strategies for rebuilding your life and rediscovering your true self.

Rebuilding Your Life

Self-Care as a Priority: Self-care is your foundation for healing. Prioritize your physical, emotional, and mental well-being. This includes getting adequate rest, eating healthily, and exercising regularly.

Embracing Emotional Healing: Allow yourself to grieve and process the emotional scars from the narcissistic relationship. Seeking therapy or counseling can provide a safe space to work through complex emotions.

Reconnecting with Your Interests: Rekindle your passions and hobbies. Engaging in activities that bring you joy and fulfillment can help rebuild your self-esteem.

Support System: Lean on your support network. Family, friends, or support groups can provide invaluable emotional support and understanding during your healing journey.

Rediscovering Your True Self

Self-Reflection: Take time to reflect on your values, goals, and personal identity. What are the aspects of yourself that may have been lost or overshadowed during the relationship?

Defining Boundaries: Set clear boundaries in your interactions with others to protect your well-being and autonomy. Learn to say no without guilt.

Reclaiming Independence: Rebuilding your sense of self-reliance is vital. This may involve pursuing further education, career development, or personal growth.

Mindfulness and Meditation: Practices like mindfulness and meditation can help you stay grounded in the present and regain a sense of inner peace.

Therapeutic Support

Therapy is a valuable resource in the healing and self-discovery process. Therapists with expertise in narcissistic abuse recovery can guide you through the emotional complexities of rebuilding your life. Additionally, therapy can help you address any trauma or unresolved issues from your past.

Recovery from a narcissistic relationship can be seen as an opportunity for profound self-discovery. As you heal and rebuild, you have the chance to uncover your true self, free from the constraints and manipulation of the past. This journey is about finding your strength, resilience, and authenticity.

8.3 Post-Narcissistic Stress Disorder (PNSD)

Recovery from a narcissistic relationship can often involve facing a unique set of challenges, including what is sometimes referred to as Post-Narcissistic Stress Disorder (PNSD). This chapter explores the characteristics of PNSD, coping strategies, and how to overcome its impact on your life.

Post-Narcissistic Stress Disorder is not an officially recognized diagnosis, but it's a term commonly used to describe the psychological and emotional distress that can follow narcissistic abuse. Characteristics of PNSD may include:

Intrusive Thoughts: Recurrent and distressing thoughts about the narcissist, the abuse, or the relationship.

Hyperarousal: Persistent feelings of anxiety, fear, and hypervigilance, often stemming from the constant need to anticipate and manage the narcissist's moods and reactions.

Avoidance: Avoiding places, people, or situations that remind you of the narcissistic relationship.

Emotional Numbness: Feeling emotionally detached, as if you've lost the ability to connect with your own emotions or the emotions of others.

Nightmares and Sleep Disturbances: Frequent nightmares or difficulties falling and staying asleep.

Coping with PNSD

Coping with PNSD involves acknowledging its existence and actively working toward healing:

Therapy and Counseling: Seek professional help from a therapist who specializes in narcissistic abuse recovery. Therapy can provide you with the tools to address and manage the emotional aftermath.

Self-Care: Prioritize self-care practices to reduce stress and anxiety. Engage in relaxation techniques such as meditation, deep breathing, and mindfulness.

Building a Support System: Lean on friends and family who understand your experiences. Support groups with individuals who've gone through similar situations can also be beneficial.

Processing Trauma: Address any unresolved trauma through therapy or support groups. Releasing repressed emotions can be a vital part of recovery.

Setting Healthy Boundaries: Learn to set and enforce healthy boundaries, not only in your current relationships but also within yourself.

Rebuilding Self-Esteem: Work on rebuilding self-esteem and self-worth that may have been eroded during the narcissistic relationship.

Recovery from PNSD is a deeply personal journey. It's important to remember that healing is possible, and while the road may be challenging, it leads to a life free from the impact of narcissistic abuse. In the following section, we will explore strategies for finding closure and moving forward, ultimately thriving after the experience of a narcissistic relationship.

8.4 *Rebuilding Relationships and Trust*

Recovering from the aftermath of a narcissistic relationship not only involves self-healing but also rebuilding connections with others and learning to trust again. This chapter delves into the complexities of rebuilding relationships and trust after narcissistic abuse.

Narcissistic abuse often leaves deep scars on your ability to connect with others. You may find yourself questioning your judgment, second-guessing people's intentions, or struggling with intimacy. Understanding that these challenges are a common part of the recovery process is the first step toward healing.

Rebuilding Trust in Relationships

Rebuilding trust after narcissistic abuse can be a gradual and cautious process:

Self-Trust: Start by rebuilding trust in yourself. Learn to trust your instincts and judgment, acknowledging that they were eroded during the narcissistic relationship.

Setting Boundaries: Reevaluate and establish healthy boundaries in your relationships. Clear boundaries are crucial to feeling safe and respected.

Transparent Communication: Open and honest communication is key. Discuss your fears, insecurities, and expectations with your loved ones.

Take Your Time: Rebuilding trust isn't a race. It's okay to take your time before trusting others completely. Genuine friends and loved ones will understand and respect your pace.

Reconnecting with Loved Ones

Reconnecting with family and friends who may have been pushed away during your narcissistic relationship can be a rewarding aspect of healing:

Apologize and Forgive: If you've distanced yourself from loved ones during the abusive relationship, offer genuine apologies and seek forgiveness.

Rebuild Bridges: Take small steps to rebuild connections. This might involve sharing your experiences and emotions with them.

Supportive Relationships: Surround yourself with supportive and understanding individuals who prioritize your healing journey.

Navigating New Relationships

As you heal, you may consider entering new relationships. Be mindful of the following:

Red Flags: Learn from the past by recognizing early signs of narcissism or abusive behavior in potential partners.

Take It Slow: Don't rush into new relationships. Get to know someone well before fully committing.

Communication: Be open about your past experiences and the impact they've had on you.

Healing Together

If you're in a relationship with someone who has also experienced narcissistic abuse, consider healing together. Joint therapy or support groups can provide a safe space for recovery.

The Road to Trust and Healthy Relationships

Rebuilding relationships and trust after narcissistic abuse is an essential part of your recovery journey. It may be challenging, but it's a transformative process that can lead to stronger, more authentic, and healthier connections with others. This chapter aims to guide you through the complexities of restoring trust in yourself and the world around you.

Chapter 9: Professional Help and Interventions

9.1 Therapy and Counseling Options

When dealing with a narcissist or recovering from narcissistic abuse, seeking professional help and interventions can be a crucial step toward healing. This chapter explores various therapy and counseling options available to individuals navigating these challenging situations.

The Role of Therapy in Narcissistic Abuse Recovery

Therapy can provide an essential lifeline for those dealing with narcissism in any capacity. Whether you're trying to cope with a narcissistic partner, heal from a past relationship, or address narcissistic traits within yourself, therapy offers a safe and supportive environment. Here are some therapy and counseling options to consider:

Individual Therapy: Psychodynamic Therapy: This approach delves into unconscious thoughts and behaviors, often helping individuals understand how past experiences shape their present relationships.

Cognitive-Behavioral Therapy (CBT): CBT can be effective in addressing thought patterns and behaviors that stem from narcissistic abuse. It promotes healthier responses to triggers.

Trauma Therapy: If you've experienced severe emotional or physical abuse, trauma-focused therapy, such as Eye Movement Desensitization and Reprocessing (EMDR), can help you process and heal from traumatic experiences.

Person-Centered Therapy: This type of therapy focuses on your self-acceptance, personal growth, and self-actualization.

Couples or Relationship Counseling:
Couples Therapy: If you're in a relationship with a narcissist, couples therapy can provide a structured and mediated environment to address relationship issues.

Family Therapy: When narcissism affects family dynamics, family therapy can be a helpful approach to improve communication and understanding.

Group Therapy: Narcissistic Abuse Support Groups: Joining support groups with individuals who've had similar experiences can provide a sense of community, validation, and healing.
Online Therapy:

Teletherapy: Convenient and accessible, online therapy platforms offer various therapeutic approaches, making it easier for individuals to find the right therapist for their needs.

Self-Help and Resources:

Books and Workbooks: Many self-help books and workbooks are designed to aid individuals in understanding and recovering from narcissistic abuse.

Websites and Forums: Online resources, forums, and websites can provide information, advice, and a platform for sharing experiences with others.

The Importance of Finding the Right Therapist

Finding a therapist who specializes in narcissistic abuse or narcissistic personality disorder (NPD) is essential. It's crucial that you feel comfortable and understood by your therapist. Don't hesitate to interview potential therapists to ensure that you're making the right choice for your healing journey.

Therapy and counseling are often integral parts of a comprehensive healing plan when dealing with narcissism, whether you're navigating a narcissistic relationship, leaving one, or recovering from its effects. In this chapter, we explore these therapy and counseling options, helping you make informed choices to support your healing process.

9.2 Family Interventions

Dealing with narcissism within a family can be particularly challenging. This chapter addresses family interventions and therapeutic strategies to help mend relationships and foster healthier dynamics.

Recognizing the Impact of Narcissism on Families

Narcissism often leaves a profound impact on family dynamics. Whether it's a narcissistic parent, sibling, or child, the consequences of narcissistic behavior can be far-reaching. Here, we explore various interventions aimed at restoring balance within the family:

Family Therapy: Understanding the Narcissistic Family System: Family therapy can help members comprehend how narcissism has shaped their family system. It explores the roles and behaviors of each family member, shedding light on the patterns that have emerged.

Improving Communication: A significant aspect of family therapy is enhancing communication within the family. It teaches healthy communication skills, enabling family members to express themselves effectively and empathetically.

Setting Boundaries: Establishing and maintaining boundaries is critical when dealing with narcissistic family members. Family therapy helps individuals define and maintain these boundaries without causing further conflict.

Interventions for Children:
Child Therapy: If you suspect a child in the family is dealing with narcissistic parents, child therapy can provide a safe space for them to express their feelings and develop healthy coping mechanisms.

Strategies for Partners and Spouses:
Partner Support Groups: If you are the partner of a narcissist, support groups provide a platform for sharing experiences and receiving advice from others who have gone through similar situations.

Couples Therapy: Couples therapy can help you and your partner navigate the challenges of living with or being in a relationship with a narcissist. It often involves improving communication, setting boundaries, and addressing relationship issues.

Understanding Enablers and Codependency:
Breaking the Cycle: Many family members unknowingly enable narcissistic behaviors or struggle with codependency. Family therapy addresses these dynamics and helps family members understand and break the cycle.

Embracing the Healing Journey

Family interventions require a willingness to change and grow together. While it may be challenging to initiate this process, it's essential for fostering healthier family relationships. This chapter explores the various family interventions available, empowering you to navigate the complexities of narcissism within your family while working towards healing and healthier connections.

9.3 Legal Considerations

Navigating a relationship with a narcissist may sometimes require legal action or protection, especially in cases involving abuse, manipulation, or threats. This chapter delves into the legal aspects you should consider when dealing with a narcissist.

Understanding Legal Concerns in Narcissistic Relationships

Narcissistic relationships can take a significant toll on one's emotional and even physical well-being. In some instances, the issues may escalate to a point where legal intervention is necessary. Below are the legal considerations to be aware of:

Domestic Violence and Restraining Orders: Recognizing Domestic Abuse: If you're a victim of domestic violence or abuse at the hands of a narcissist, it's crucial to understand the signs and severity of the situation.

Seeking a Restraining Order: A restraining order, also known as a protective order, can provide legal protection by requiring the narcissist to maintain a specific distance from you, your home, or workplace.

Child Custody and Legal Rights:
Child Custody Battles: In cases where children are involved, navigating child custody disputes with a narcissistic partner can be especially challenging. This section outlines the legal aspects of child custody and offers insights into managing the process.

Divorce and Separation:
Preparing for Divorce: Divorcing a narcissist can be fraught with conflict. Understanding the legal steps, documentation, and support you need is vital.

Collaborative Law and Mediation: Exploring alternative dispute resolution methods, such as collaborative law and mediation, can reduce the hostility of divorce proceedings.

Privacy and Online Safety:
Online Harassment and Privacy Invasion: Narcissists might engage in online harassment or invade your privacy. This section provides information on how to protect yourself legally.
Protective Orders and Legal Rights:

Stalking Orders: In cases of stalking or harassment, you can seek a stalking order to prohibit the narcissist from contacting you or coming near your home or workplace.

Divorce and Legal Consultation: Legal representation is crucial when navigating complex divorce or child custody cases with a narcissist. Seeking legal consultation can help you understand your rights and options.

This chapter emphasizes the importance of understanding your legal rights and seeking professional legal advice when necessary. Dealing with a narcissist can be a challenging legal journey, and the insights provided in this chapter are designed to help you protect yourself and your rights during this process.

9.4 Support Groups and Resources

While navigating the complexities of dealing with a narcissist, it's crucial to have a strong support system in place. In this chapter, we explore the value of support groups and various resources available to aid you in your journey.

The Power of Support Groups

Support groups can be invaluable for individuals dealing with narcissistic relationships. These groups provide a safe space to share experiences, gain insight, and offer emotional support. Key points covered include:

Joining a Support Group: Discover the benefits of joining a support group tailored to those dealing with narcissistic relationships. These groups can be in-person or online.

Finding the Right Group: Learn how to find a support group that best fits your needs and preferences. This may include considering the specific focus, meeting format, and group dynamics.

Online Support Forums: Explore the multitude of online forums and communities where individuals share their experiences, offer advice, and seek solace.

Group Dynamics and Norms: Understand the dynamics of support groups, including the importance of anonymity, confidentiality, and respectful communication.

Resources for Coping and Recovery

This section delves into the array of resources available to support you during your journey. Topics covered include:

Books and Literature: Recommended reading materials and books that delve into narcissism and its impact on relationships.

Professional Therapists and Counselors: Guidance on how to find a qualified therapist or counselor with experience in narcissistic abuse and recovery.

Online Resources: An overview of credible websites, articles, and online platforms that provide insights, strategies, and expert advice.

Mental Health Apps: An introduction to apps designed to aid in emotional healing and self-care, as well as improve mental health.

Self-Care Strategies within Support Networks

Self-care is a cornerstone of healing when dealing with narcissistic relationships. This section offers guidance on integrating self-care into your journey, including:

Balancing Empathy: Finding a balance between empathy and self-preservation when dealing with a narcissist.

Creating a Supportive Environment: Fostering a nurturing environment in which you can heal and regain emotional strength.

Setting Boundaries: Understanding the importance of boundaries and implementing them to protect your well-being.

This chapter highlights the significance of professional help and support groups during your journey to manage a narcissist. By leveraging these resources, you can better understand the dynamics of narcissism, cope with its effects, and find a path to healing and recovery.

Chapter 10: Coping with Co-Parenting

10.1 Parenting Strategies with a Narcissistic Ex

Co-parenting with a narcissistic ex-partner can be an incredibly challenging and emotionally draining experience. In this chapter, we explore effective parenting strategies and coping mechanisms to ensure the well-being of your children and yourself while dealing with a narcissistic co-parent.

Understanding the Challenge

Co-parenting with a narcissist often presents unique challenges due to their need for control, manipulation, and lack of empathy. This section delves into the specifics of the challenge, including:

The Narcissistic Co-Parent: Understanding the characteristics and behaviors of a narcissistic co-parent.

Impact on Children: Recognizing how co-parenting with a narcissist can affect your children's emotional and psychological well-being.

Legal Considerations: Exploring the legal aspects of co-parenting and custody arrangements when a narcissistic ex is involved.

Effective Parenting Strategies

This section focuses on practical strategies to navigate co-parenting with a narcissistic ex-partner. Key topics include:

Parallel Parenting: The concept of parallel parenting and how it can help reduce conflict and tension.

Setting Boundaries: Establishing clear and healthy boundaries with your co-parent to protect yourself and your children.

Communication Techniques: Strategies for maintaining necessary communication while minimizing conflict and emotional distress.

Documentation: The importance of keeping records of interactions and incidents related to co-parenting.

Fostering Emotional Resilience

Coping with a narcissistic co-parent can take an emotional toll. This section discusses how to foster emotional resilience during this process:

Self-Care: The importance of self-care and its role in emotional resilience.

Support Systems: Building and maintaining a support system to provide emotional assistance.

Emotional Regulation: Techniques for managing your emotional responses to challenging situations.

Professional Help: Knowing when to seek professional guidance for yourself or your children.

Minimizing the Impact on Children

In this section, we address ways to minimize the impact of co-parenting with a narcissist on your children:

Healthy Coping Mechanisms: Encouraging your children to develop healthy coping strategies.

Empathy and Understanding: Teaching your children to understand and handle difficult emotions and behaviors.

Providing Stability: The importance of providing stability and consistency within your household.

<u>*Legal Considerations and Resources*</u>

This section provides an overview of legal considerations and resources to help you navigate co-parenting with a narcissist:

Custody Agreements: Understanding different types of custody agreements and their implications.

Mediation and Legal Support: The role of mediation and legal support in resolving co-parenting disputes.

Supportive Resources: An introduction to books, articles, and support groups that cater to co-parents dealing with narcissistic ex-partners.

By employing effective parenting strategies, fostering emotional resilience, and understanding the legal aspects, you can empower yourself as a co-parent and provide your children with a stable, nurturing environment, even in the presence of a narcissistic ex-partner.

10.2 The Impact on Children

Co-parenting with a narcissistic ex-spouse not only affects you but also has a significant impact on your children. In this section, we delve into the various ways in which co-parenting with a narcissist influences children and discuss strategies to mitigate the negative consequences.

The Emotional Toll on Children

Children of narcissistic co-parents often bear the emotional brunt of the situation. Some of the emotional challenges they may face include:

Confusion: The erratic behavior of a narcissistic parent can leave children confused about what to expect and how to react.

Anxiety and Fear: Narcissistic parents can be unpredictable, leading to anxiety and fear in their children.

Low Self-Esteem: Constant criticism and emotional manipulation may erode a child's self-esteem and self-worth.

Role Reversal: Children might be forced into a role reversal, where they become caretakers for their narcissistic parent.

Coping Mechanisms for Children

To help children cope with the impact of co-parenting with a narcissist, consider the following strategies:

Open Communication: Encourage children to express their feelings, fears, and concerns about the co-parenting situation.

Validation: Acknowledge and validate their emotions, letting them know that their feelings are understood and accepted.

Psychoeducation: Educate children about narcissism and its effects, tailored to their age and maturity level.

Therapeutic Support: Explore the option of therapy or counseling for children to provide them with a safe space to address their emotions.

Maintaining Stability

Consistency and stability are crucial for children who are navigating the tumultuous waters of co-parenting with a narcissist:

Routine: Establishing a predictable routine can help children feel secure and grounded.

Supportive Environment: Create an environment that is free from conflict and emotional turmoil.

Healthy Coping: Teach children healthy coping mechanisms to deal with the stress and emotions they may experience.

Empowering Children

Children are more resilient than we often give them credit for. By providing them with the tools, support, and understanding they need, you can empower them to thrive despite the challenges they face:

Encourage Independence: Foster a sense of independence and self-sufficiency in children, ensuring they feel capable and confident.

Positive Role Models: Offer children positive role models and access to supportive relationships outside the immediate family.

Reassurance: Regularly reassure your children of your love and support, emphasizing that they are not responsible for the behaviors of their narcissistic parent.

Remember, your children's well-being is of paramount importance in the co-parenting journey, and with the right strategies and support, they can emerge from this situation with resilience and strength.

10.3 Legal Custody and Co-Parenting Agreements

Navigating the complexities of co-parenting with a narcissist often requires a well-structured legal framework. In this section, we explore the legal aspects of custody arrangements and co-parenting agreements and how they can help create a stable and secure environment for your children.

Legal custody refers to the authority to make decisions about your child's upbringing, including education, healthcare, and religious upbringing. There are two primary types:

Joint Legal Custody: Both parents share decision-making responsibilities, and they must work together to make major life decisions for the child.

Sole Legal Custody: One parent has the exclusive authority to make decisions concerning the child's well-being. This can be challenging to obtain and is typically reserved for cases where one parent is deemed unfit.

Creating a Co-Parenting Agreement

A well-crafted co-parenting agreement can serve as a crucial tool for reducing conflicts and ensuring the best interests of your children. Here's what it typically includes:

Custody Arrangements: Outlining the physical and legal custody arrangement, specifying visitation schedules and decision-making processes.

Communication Plan: Detailing how parents will communicate about matters concerning the child, including the preferred method and frequency.

Dispute Resolution: Establishing a procedure for resolving disputes and conflicts that may arise during co-parenting.

Child Support: Addressing financial responsibilities, including child support payments, health insurance, and educational expenses.

Holidays and Special Occasions: Determining how holidays, birthdays, and special events will be divided between co-parents.

Relocation: Setting guidelines if one parent intends to relocate, ensuring it doesn't disrupt the child's life.

Consistency and Stability: Prioritizing the child's routine, including schooling and extracurricular activities.

Mediation and Legal Support

In situations where cooperation is challenging, mediation can be a valuable resource. A trained mediator can assist in reaching compromises, improving communication, and ultimately fostering a healthier co-parenting relationship.

Legal support may also be necessary, especially if the narcissistic parent refuses to comply with the co-parenting agreement or if you need to modify the agreement to better serve your child's interests.

Legal custody arrangements play a vital role in co-parenting situations, ensuring that both parents understand their roles and responsibilities.

A well-structured co-parenting agreement can mitigate conflicts and create a stable environment for your children.

Mediation and legal support are valuable resources for resolving disputes and enforcing co-parenting agreements.

Remember, while legal custody and co-parenting agreements are essential, the well-being of your children remains the ultimate focus. These tools exist to provide a stable and secure environment for them during the challenging journey of co-parenting with a narcissist.

10.4 Emotional Support for Children

In the intricate dance of co-parenting with a narcissist, it's essential to focus not only on the logistics but also on the emotional well-being of your children. This chapter delves into the crucial aspects of providing emotional support to your kids during these challenging times.

Understanding the Emotional Impact

Children caught in the crossfire of a co-parenting relationship with a narcissist can experience a wide range of emotions. They may feel confused, anxious, and torn between two worlds. Recognizing and addressing their emotional needs is paramount to their well-being.

Communication and Validation

Open and honest communication with your children is a cornerstone of emotional support. Encourage them to express their feelings, questions, and concerns. Let them know their emotions are valid, and it's okay to feel the way they do.

Stability and Routine

In a co-parenting arrangement, children benefit greatly from stability and routine. Both households should strive to maintain consistency in rules, expectations, and daily schedules. This predictability can provide a sense of security.

Reassurance and Rebuilding Trust

Children may lose trust in relationships due to the conflicts they witness between their parents. It's crucial to reassure them of your love and commitment to their well-being. Rebuilding trust may take time, patience, and consistency.

Child-Centered Coping Strategies

Teaching your children healthy coping strategies is essential. Encourage them to express themselves through creative outlets, sports, or counseling if needed. These activities can serve as effective emotional outlets.

Counseling and Therapy

In some cases, professional counseling or therapy may be necessary for children dealing with the emotional toll of co-parenting with a narcissist. A trained therapist can provide them with coping mechanisms and a safe space to express their feelings.

Balancing Their Loyalties

Children caught in the middle of parental conflicts may feel the need to choose sides. Emphasize that they don't have to choose between their parents and that it's acceptable to love both. Your support in maintaining these relationships can alleviate their emotional burden.

Teamwork with the Co-Parent

While it can be incredibly challenging, collaborating with the narcissistic co-parent to provide emotional support to your children is essential. Try to maintain a united front when it comes to their well-being.

Conclusion

Coping with co-parenting and nurturing your children's emotional health in the presence of a narcissist is a formidable task. However, by providing emotional support, fostering open communication, and maintaining stability, you can significantly mitigate the emotional impact of the situation on your children. Remember, your dedication to their well-being can make a world of difference as they navigate this challenging terrain.

Chapter 11: The Journey to Empowerment

11.1 Self-Empowerment and Growth

This chapter marks a pivotal point in your journey of managing a narcissist in your life. It focuses on self-empowerment and personal growth, as these are fundamental aspects of regaining control over your life and building a better future.

Understanding Self-Empowerment

Self-empowerment is the process of taking control of your life and making choices that align with your values, desires, and well-being. It's about realizing your worth and believing in your ability to effect positive change.

Recognizing the Need for Self-Empowerment

In situations involving narcissists, individuals often feel powerless or controlled. Recognizing the need for self-empowerment is the first step toward breaking free from the chains of manipulation and regaining control over your life.

Boosting Self-Esteem and Confidence

Low self-esteem is a common side effect of dealing with a narcissist. This section explores strategies for rebuilding your self-esteem and confidence, which are critical for self-empowerment.

Setting Personal Boundaries

Establishing and maintaining healthy boundaries is crucial for self-empowerment. Learn how to define and communicate your boundaries effectively while respecting the boundaries of others.

Taking Ownership of Your Choices

Taking ownership of your choices empowers you to reclaim control over your life. This section delves into strategies for making proactive decisions aligned with your goals and values.

Embracing Personal Growth

Personal growth is a continuous journey. Explore ways to develop new skills, broaden your knowledge, and expand your horizons. Embracing personal growth is key to self-empowerment.

Self-Care and Well-Being

Prioritizing self-care and well-being is an essential aspect of self-empowerment. Discover effective self-care practices and strategies for maintaining your physical and mental health.

Building a Support System

Having a support system is vital on the path to self-empowerment. This section discusses how to build and nurture a network of friends, family, or support groups who can aid in your personal growth.

Facing and Overcoming Challenges

Self-empowerment doesn't eliminate challenges, but it equips you to face them with resilience. Learn strategies for dealing with obstacles and maintaining your newfound sense of empowerment.

Goal Setting and Achievement

Setting and achieving goals are fundamental to self-empowerment. This chapter provides guidance on setting realistic and inspiring goals that can lead to personal growth and fulfillment.

Conclusion

Self-empowerment is the cornerstone of your journey toward managing a narcissist effectively and finding personal growth and fulfillment. By understanding your worth, setting boundaries, embracing personal growth, and fostering a robust support system, you can regain control over your life and steer it in a direction that aligns with your values and aspirations. This chapter is your roadmap to empowerment and self-discovery.

11.2 Thriving Beyond Narcissism

This section of the chapter focuses on not just surviving but thriving beyond the influence of narcissism. It's about discovering a life filled with purpose, happiness, and personal growth once the narcissist's grip has been loosened.

Reclaiming Your Identity

Narcissists often manipulate and control their victims to the point where they lose their sense of self. You'll learn how to rediscover and reclaim your identity, interests, and passions.

Rediscovering Your Dreams

In the process of thriving beyond narcissism, it's essential to revisit your dreams and aspirations. This section will guide you in rekindling your passions and setting new, achievable goals.

Building Healthy Relationships

As you emerge from the shadow of narcissism, it's time to focus on building and nurturing healthy relationships. This includes learning how to trust again, communicate effectively, and create bonds based on mutual respect.

Parenting After Narcissism

If you have children, co-parenting with a narcissist can be particularly challenging. This section offers advice on promoting a stable and nurturing environment for your children as they recover from the narcissistic influence.

Advocacy and Sharing Your Experience

Many survivors choose to use their experiences to help others. This section explores advocacy and the various ways you can share your journey to inspire, educate, and support others facing similar challenges.

Thriving Beyond Narcissism: Real Stories

Hearing from individuals who have thrived beyond narcissism can be empowering. This section includes real-life stories of survivors who have emerged stronger, more confident, and happier after their experiences.

Creating a Vision for Your Future

Setting a clear vision for your future is a crucial part of thriving. You'll learn how to create a vision that reflects your values, desires, and the life you want to lead beyond the influence of narcissism.

The Role of Professional Help

Professional guidance and support can be instrumental in the process of thriving. We'll discuss how therapy, counseling, and other forms of assistance can help you reach your full potential.

The Ongoing Journey

Thriving beyond narcissism is an ongoing journey. This section emphasizes the importance of continuous self-care, personal growth, and maintaining your support network.

Closing Thoughts

Thriving beyond narcissism is not only possible but also an achievable reality. This chapter has equipped you with the knowledge and tools needed to not just recover from narcissistic abuse but to thrive in all areas of your life. As you continue on this journey, remember that you are strong, resilient, and capable of creating a life filled with happiness, purpose, and personal growth.

11.3 Reclaiming Your Life

Reclaiming your life is the ultimate goal in your journey to empowerment. It involves rebuilding, recovering, and moving forward with newfound strength and confidence.

Breaking Free from Emotional Chains

This section addresses the emotional scars left by narcissistic abuse. It delves into the process of healing, forgiving, and letting go of the past, helping you break free from emotional chains.

Rebuilding Trust in Yourself

Narcissistic abuse can erode self-esteem and self-trust. You'll discover techniques for rebuilding trust in yourself, your instincts, and your decision-making abilities.

Healthy Lifestyle and Self-Care

Maintaining a healthy lifestyle and practicing self-care are vital aspects of reclaiming your life. This section explores the significance of physical and mental well-being in your empowerment journey.

Forgiveness and Closure

Forgiveness doesn't mean condoning the narcissist's actions but releasing the burden of anger and resentment. This chapter helps you navigate the path to forgiveness and find closure.

Setting New Boundaries

Healthy boundaries are essential for preventing future toxic relationships. This section offers guidance on establishing and maintaining boundaries that protect your emotional and mental well-being.

Reconnecting with Joy

The journey to empowerment is about rediscovering joy and happiness. You'll explore activities and practices that bring joy back into your life.

Financial Recovery

Narcissistic relationships can leave a financial toll. This section provides strategies for financial recovery and building a secure future.

Reclaiming Your Independence

Independence is a key aspect of empowerment. This chapter discusses how to regain your independence in all areas of life, from personal to financial.

Healing Through Creativity

Creativity can be a powerful tool for healing. Whether through art, writing, or other creative outlets, this section encourages you to express and heal.

Your Support Network

Building a strong support network is crucial in your journey. This chapter explores how to find and maintain healthy, supportive relationships.

The Importance of Gratitude

Practicing gratitude is a key element in your journey to empowerment. You'll learn how acknowledging the positive aspects of life can foster resilience.

Celebrating Milestones

Celebrate your achievements and milestones along the way. This section will guide you in acknowledging and appreciating your progress.

Embracing Your New Life

Reclaiming your life is a process of transformation. This chapter emphasizes embracing your newfound strength, wisdom, and the possibilities of your future.

Final Thoughts

Reclaiming your life is a journey of healing, empowerment, and transformation. This chapter has equipped you with the knowledge and tools needed to rebuild, recover, and move forward with strength and confidence. As you continue to navigate this path, remember that your life is yours to reclaim, and you have the power to create a future filled with happiness, purpose, and self-empowerment.

Chapter 12: Looking Ahead

12.1 The Future of Narcissism

As we conclude this journey of understanding and managing narcissism, it's essential to explore what the future holds for narcissism as a concept and as a societal issue.

Evolution of Narcissism

This section delves into how the concept of narcissism has evolved over the years and how our understanding of it has changed. We'll explore how societal, cultural, and technological shifts impact narcissism.

Narcissism in the Digital Age

The digital age has introduced new platforms for narcissistic behaviors. We'll discuss the impact of social media, online dating, and digital interactions on narcissism and relationships.

Psychology and Neuroscience Advances

Advancements in psychology and neuroscience have provided insights into the narcissistic personality. This section explores how research and technology are contributing to our understanding of narcissism.

Narcissism in Pop Culture and Media

Narcissism is a recurring theme in literature, film, and media. We'll analyze the portrayal of narcissism in popular culture and its effects on public perception.

Narcissism and Gender Dynamics

This section delves into how narcissism is understood in the context of evolving gender dynamics. We'll explore how changes in traditional gender roles are influencing narcissistic behaviors.

The Ongoing Struggle for Empathy

The future of managing narcissism hinges on society's ability to cultivate empathy. This chapter examines efforts to enhance empathy and compassion in relationships and communities.

Educational Initiatives

Education plays a vital role in addressing narcissism. We'll discuss how educational institutions and programs are adapting to teach emotional intelligence, relationship skills, and empathy.

Preventing Narcissistic Abuse

Preventing narcissistic abuse is a key focus for the future. We'll explore strategies, awareness campaigns, and legal measures aimed at protecting potential victims.

Rehabilitation and Recovery

Rehabilitation programs for individuals with narcissistic traits are emerging. This section examines their effectiveness and their potential impact on reducing narcissistic behaviors.

Balancing Self-Empowerment and Selflessness

Finding a balance between self-empowerment and selflessness is vital. This chapter discusses how individuals can navigate this balance in their lives and relationships.

Concluding Thoughts

The future of narcissism is a complex and evolving landscape. It requires ongoing efforts in understanding, prevention, and healing. As we look ahead, it's essential to remain vigilant, compassionate, and committed to creating healthier, more empathetic communities and relationships. The journey to manage narcissism continues, but with knowledge, awareness, and support, we can navigate the path toward a more empathetic and emotionally intelligent future.

12.2 Breaking the Cycle

As we continue to explore the future of narcissism, this section is dedicated to breaking the cycle of narcissistic behaviors and their impact on individuals and society.

Understanding the Cycle

To break the cycle, it's essential to first understand it. This section delves into the repetitive patterns of narcissistic behaviors, the emotional toll they take on victims, and the societal implications.

Healing for Victims

For those who have experienced narcissistic abuse, healing is a crucial step. We discuss the various therapeutic approaches, support systems, and strategies to aid survivors in their journey towards recovery.

Supporting Empathy Development

Breaking the cycle of narcissism involves fostering empathy. We explore practical ways to nurture empathy in children and adults, emphasizing its role in preventing narcissistic tendencies.

Teaching Healthy Relationship Dynamics

Education is a powerful tool in preventing the perpetuation of narcissistic behaviors. This section discusses how teaching healthy relationship dynamics can break the cycle at its root.

Interventions and Accountability

Accountability is necessary to break the cycle. We examine interventions, legal measures, and community-based actions that hold narcissists accountable for their actions.

Preventing Narcissistic Behavior in Future Generations

Breaking the cycle necessitates efforts to prevent narcissistic behaviors from being passed down to future generations. This section outlines strategies for raising emotionally intelligent and empathetic children.

Promoting Empathetic Leadership

In workplaces and society, promoting empathetic leadership can disrupt the cycle of narcissism. We discuss leadership models that prioritize empathy and their potential impact.

Redefining Success

Societal success metrics often fuel narcissistic behaviors. We explore how redefining success can shift the focus towards values such as kindness, compassion, and cooperation.

Global Efforts

Narcissism is a global issue. We'll look at international efforts and collaborative initiatives aimed at breaking the cycle and fostering greater global empathy.

Empowering Communities

Communities play a vital role in breaking the cycle of narcissism. This section emphasizes the importance of community support, awareness, and healing.

A Compassionate Future

Breaking the cycle of narcissism is a collective endeavor that requires compassion and dedication. As we look ahead, the goal is to create a future where narcissism no longer defines our relationships and communities. Instead, we aim for a world where empathy, emotional intelligence, and healthy connections thrive.

Concluding Thoughts

Breaking the cycle of narcissism is an ambitious but necessary goal. It's a journey that demands commitment, education, awareness, and compassion. As we conclude our exploration of narcissism, remember that change is possible. The future holds the promise of healthier, more empathetic individuals, relationships, workplaces, and societies. Breaking the cycle is a shared responsibility, and with concerted efforts, we can look forward to a future marked by genuine empathy, kindness, and emotional growth.

12.3 Promoting Empathy and Mental Health

In our final exploration of the future of narcissism, we turn our attention to the critical role of empathy and mental health in reshaping relationships, society, and individual well-being.

The Power of Empathy

Empathy is a cornerstone of healthy relationships and a key component in breaking the cycle of narcissism. In this section, we delve into the transformative power of empathy and its far-reaching effects.

Emotional Intelligence

Promoting empathy begins with developing emotional intelligence. We discuss how emotional intelligence equips individuals to understand and manage their emotions while fostering empathy in their interactions with others.

Educational Initiatives

Education is a powerful tool in promoting empathy and mental health. We explore how curricula that prioritize emotional intelligence and empathy can shape the future generation's perspectives on relationships and communication.

Community Awareness

Communities can be hubs of empathy and mental health support. This section examines how community awareness programs can promote mental health, emotional well-being, and empathetic connections.

Destigmatizing Mental Health

Mental health awareness and destigmatization are crucial steps towards breaking the cycle of narcissism. We explore campaigns and initiatives that aim to normalize discussions about mental health and encourage seeking help when needed.

Supporting Survivors

For individuals who have experienced narcissistic abuse, support is essential. We discuss support networks, therapeutic approaches, and resources available to survivors to aid in their healing journey.

Preventive Mental Health

Prevention is key in promoting empathy and mental health. We discuss strategies and initiatives designed to prevent narcissistic behaviors and prioritize mental well-being in both individuals and communities.

Corporate Empathy

In workplaces, the promotion of empathy and mental health can have a profound impact on employee well-being and productivity. We explore corporate initiatives that prioritize the mental health of employees and foster empathetic leadership.

Empathy on a Global Scale

Promoting empathy transcends borders. We discuss global efforts, collaborative ventures, and international organizations dedicated to spreading empathy and mental health awareness.

Empowering Individuals

At its core, promoting empathy and mental health empowers individuals to lead healthier, more fulfilling lives. We provide practical strategies for individuals to foster empathy, manage their mental health, and build stronger connections.

A Future Marked by Empathy

As we look ahead, the future holds the promise of a world marked by empathy, emotional intelligence, and prioritization of mental health. The promotion of empathy isn't just a lofty goal; it's a practical approach to healthier, happier individuals and a more harmonious society. While the journey may be challenging, the rewards—stronger relationships, emotional well-being, and a kinder world—are worth the effort.

Concluding Thoughts

Our exploration of narcissism and its effects comes to an end with the hope that promoting empathy and mental health will be at the forefront of our collective efforts. By focusing on these aspects, we can work towards a future where narcissism is replaced with understanding, empathy, and mental well-being. As individuals and communities embrace these values, we pave

the way for a brighter and more empathetic
world.

Conclusion

In the pages of this book, we've embarked on a comprehensive journey to understand and manage narcissism in its various forms. We've delved into the depths of narcissistic behavior, the impact it has on relationships, workplaces, and society at large, and we've explored strategies for managing, coping with, and ultimately, recovering from these complex dynamics.

A Holistic Approach to Narcissism

Our journey began with a thorough examination of narcissism, from its definitions and misconceptions to the spectrum of narcissistic traits and the diagnosis of Narcissistic Personality Disorder (NPD). Understanding the origins of narcissism allowed us to challenge prevalent myths and misconceptions, laying the groundwork for a nuanced approach.

Recognizing Narcissistic Behavior

As we ventured deeper, we explored the red flags, warning signs, and covert versus overt manifestations of narcissistic behavior. Understanding the concept of narcissistic supply and distinguishing NPD from other personality disorders became our compass in navigating these intricate waters.

The Impact of Narcissism

Narcissism's pervasive influence in different spheres of life was next on our itinerary. We scrutinized its effects on relationships, the workplace, family dynamics, and broader societal and cultural contexts. The narcissistic cycle of abuse became an indispensable insight into comprehending the gravity of these dynamics.

Coping and Self-Care

In Chapter 4, we discussed strategies for self-care, including setting boundaries, maintaining emotional health, seeking support, and practicing patience and empathy. These tools empower individuals to manage their emotional well-being when confronted with narcissistic behavior.

Strategies for Managing a Narcissist

Chapter 5 offered a rich toolkit for dealing with narcissists, from effective communication techniques to navigating manipulative tactics, resolving conflicts, and employing techniques such as the Grey Rock method and the "Broken Record" approach.

Navigating Relationships

In Chapter 6, we explored how narcissism impacts romantic relationships, family dynamics, friendships, and co-parenting. These insights are invaluable for anyone seeking to maintain healthier connections in these domains.

Chapter 7 was dedicated to the implications of narcissism in professional settings. We delved into recognizing narcissism in the office, managing relationships with narcissistic bosses, dealing with narcissistic colleagues, and the interplay of narcissism and leadership.

The Recovery Journey

Chapter 8 offered guidance for those looking to leave or detach from a narcissistic relationship, embark on a path of healing and self-discovery, address post-narcissistic stress disorder (PNSD), and rebuild relationships and trust.

Professional Help and Interventions

Chapter 9 introduced therapeutic and counseling options, family interventions, legal considerations, and support groups as ways to navigate the complex terrain of narcissistic relationships.

Coping with Co-Parenting

Chapter 10 shed light on co-parenting with a narcissist, including parenting strategies, the impact on children, legal custody, and emotional support for children.

The Journey to Empowerment

Chapter 11 invited readers to embark on a journey of self-empowerment, thrive beyond narcissism, and reclaim their lives after narcissistic experiences.

Looking Ahead

In Chapter 12, we contemplated the future of narcissism, with a focus on breaking the cycle, promoting empathy and mental health, and empowering individuals and communities to foster healthier connections.

A Collective Commitment

As we conclude our comprehensive exploration of narcissism, it's essential to remember that these pages are not just an academic exercise but a call to action. The insights you've gained here empower you to make positive changes, both in your personal life and in the broader societal context.

A Path to Empathy

It's our collective responsibility to promote empathy, emotional intelligence, and mental health. By doing so, we can actively challenge and transform the narcissistic behaviors that have harmed so many. As you take this journey forward, remember that every step you take, every boundary you set, and every empathetic connection you make contributes to a world marked by understanding, kindness, and emotional well-being.

Reclaiming Your Life

You are not alone on this path. Countless others have walked it before you, and many will follow. By sharing your experiences, offering support, and advocating for empathy and mental health, you contribute to a world that's brighter, more compassionate, and more resilient.

Thank you for joining us on this journey of understanding and managing narcissism. As you step into the world armed with knowledge and empowered with empathy, remember that you are part of a growing movement towards healthier, more compassionate connections and a brighter future for all.

With this conclusion, we complete our journey through the complexities of narcissism and look ahead to a world marked by empathy, understanding, and emotional well-being.